FROM CHATBOT TO CASH COW: HOW CHATGPT CAN HELP YOU BECOME A MILLIONAIRE

YOUR ULTIMATE GUIDE TO CHATGPT MILLIONAIRE SUCCESS: BUILDING WEALTH WITH AUTOMATION AND AI

Copyright © 2023. All rights reserved.

No part of this publication may be reproduced, distributed, or transmitted in any form or by any means, including photocopying, recording, or other electronic or mechanical methods, without the prior written permission of the publisher, except in the case of brief quotations embodied in critical reviews and certain other noncommercial uses permitted by copyright law.

Legal Notice:

This book is intended for informational purposes only. The publisher and the author make no representation or warranties with respect to the accuracy, applicability, fitness, or completeness of the contents of this book. The information contained in this book is strictly for educational purposes. Therefore, if you wish to apply ideas contained in this book, you are taking full responsibility for your actions.

The author and publisher disclaim any warranties (express or implied), merchantability, or fitness for any particular purpose. The author and publisher shall in no event be held liable for any loss or other damages, including but not limited to special, incidental, consequential, or other damages. As always, the advice of a competent legal, tax, accounting or other professional should be sought.

Disclaimer:

The use of the ChatGPT platform and any information provided in this book is at your own risk. While the author has made every effort to provide accurate and up-to-date information, the author and publisher cannot guarantee the reliability, accuracy, or completeness of any information or examples provided herein. The author and publisher disclaim any responsibility for any errors, omissions, or inaccuracies that may be present in this book. In no event shall the author or publisher be liable for any damages resulting from the use or misuse of the information contained within this book or from the use of the ChatGPT platform.

Table of Contents

Introduction — 5

Chapter 1. Understanding ChatGPT and the "Make Money" Niche — 8
- Brief Overview of ChatGPT — 8
- Overview of the "Make Money" Niche — 9
- Identifying Opportunities — 11
- Examples of ChatGPT's potential impact on the niche — 13

Chapter 2. Brainstorming Business Ideas with ChatGPT — 15
- Techniques for Brainstorming — 15
- Developing Innovative Offerings — 18
- Validating and refining ideas — 21
- Real world examples and case studies — 23

Chapter 3. Crafting Business Plans and Strategies with ChatGPT — 25
- Creating business plans — 25
- Developing marketing strategies — 27
- Analyzing competitors — 29
- Examples of successful strategies — 32

Chapter 4. Content Creation with ChatGPT — 35
- Utilizing ChatGPT for content types — 35
- Crafting email campaigns — 37
- Developing sales copy — 39
- Content creation examples and case studies — 42

Chapter 5. Mastering Content Marketing with ChatGPT — 45
- Planning content marketing strategies — 45
- SEO optimization — 48
- Social media and influencer marketing — 50
- Successful content marketing examples — 53

## Chapter 6. Monitoring Performance and Analytics	56
Setting up KPIs	*56*
Leveraging ChatGPT for data analysis	*58*
Adapting and refining strategies	*60*
Performance monitoring examples	*62*

## Chapter 7. Scaling Your Business with ChatGPT	64
Identifying New Markets	*64*
Expanding product/service offerings	*66*
Building a sustainable business model	*68*
Examples of successful scaling	*70*

## Chapter 8. ChatGPT-4	73
Key differences between ChatGPT-4 and GPT-3	*73*
When to Choose ChatGPT-4 over GPT-3	*74*

## Appendix A – The Act Mode of ChatGPT	75

## Appendix B – ChatGPT Supported Writing Styles	77

## Appendix C – Bonus 200 Exclusive ChatGPT Prompts	79

## Conclusion	80

Introduction

The meteoric rise of artificial intelligence (AI) has set off a sea of transformations in the way businesses operate and people interact with technology. ChatGPT, a masterful natural language processing model crafted by OpenAI, stands out as one of the most awe-inspiring AI feats. Its capacity to comprehend and generate human-like text could transform many facets of business, including the lucrative "make money" niche, into a perplexing and unpredictable arena.

The "make money" niche brims with an array of prospects, ranging from online entrepreneurship and affiliate marketing to freelance work and investment strategies. With technology evolving at an accelerated pace and the internet landscape continuously shifting, the "make money" niche diversifies and grows, offering a wealth of opportunities for those seeking financial success. For instance, ChatGPT empowers e-commerce store owners to create mind-boggling product descriptions and marketing materials, affiliate marketers to generate captivating content for their target audience, and freelancers to brainstorm ingenious ideas for new projects and services.

This book aspires to be a comprehensive guide to unleashing the full range of ChatGPT's capabilities in generating inventive business ideas and gripping content in the "make money" niche. By centering on ChatGPT's chat interface, we aim to explore how users can harness the full power of this AI tool in unpredictable and thrilling ways that do not necessitate API integration, making it more accessible to a wider audience.

Throughout the book, we will delve into how ChatGPT can help you come up with dazzling and unexpected business ideas, construct impactful marketing strategies, and generate various types of content, such as riveting blog posts and social media updates, as well as persuasive email campaigns and sales copy. Through innumerable examples and case studies, we will demonstrate how ChatGPT can empower both fledgling and seasoned entrepreneurs to conquer the "make money" niche.

Imagine the case of an aspiring entrepreneur who dreams of launching a personal finance blog. With ChatGPT, they can unlock a wave of creativity that leads to unique, thought-provoking blog post ideas, unconventional marketing strategies, and search engine optimization (SEO) techniques that defy expectations. Similarly, a dropshipping company owner could use ChatGPT to craft product descriptions that are bursting with burstiness and perplexity, email campaigns that stun their target audience, and social media content that is both quirky and engaging.

This book serves two primary functions. First, it aims to familiarize readers with ChatGPT's extraordinary potential as a tool for idea generation and content creation. Second, it serves as a step-by-step guide to using the chat interface to unlock new vistas of opportunities and drive success in the "make money" niche. We firmly believe that by infusing the power of AI with human creativity, ChatGPT can enable users to unlock new levels of creativity and drive success in their ventures.

Join us on an exhilarating journey into the fascinating world of ChatGPT and its mind-bending applications in the "make money" niche. This book is not for the faint-hearted - it's for those who are willing to challenge the status quo, shatter boundaries, and explore the unknown. We aim to spark your curiosity and imagination, while also equipping you with the knowledge and techniques you need to thrive in this hyper-competitive landscape. Let's take a deep dive into ChatGPT and unleash its full potential to help you leave your mark in the "make money" niche.

In the coming chapters, we'll guide you through the maze of ChatGPT's capabilities and show you how to use them to generate creative business ideas, develop comprehensive business plans, and create stunning content that resonates with your audience. With real-world examples and case studies that push the boundaries of what's possible, you'll gain invaluable insights into how ChatGPT can transform your approach to business and content creation in the "make money" niche.

This book arms you with the tools and techniques you need to harness the full power of ChatGPT, whether you're an aspiring entrepreneur looking to build a wildly successful online business, an affiliate marketer seeking to supercharge your content strategy, or a freelance professional looking to expand your service offerings in new and exciting ways.

We understand that the world of AI can be a little intimidating, but we're confident that ChatGPT's transformative potential is worth the effort. You'll quickly become a master of the chat interface as you work your way through the book, unlocking ChatGPT's full potential to generate compelling ideas and content for your "make money" business.

We encourage you to dive in and put the strategies and techniques outlined in this book into practice as soon as possible. By actively engaging with ChatGPT, you'll gain first-hand experience of its potential to revolutionize your business and accelerate your path to success in the "make money" niche.

So, what are you waiting for? Join us on this thrilling adventure into the world of ChatGPT and the "make money" niche, and let's push the boundaries of what's possible together. With ChatGPT by your side and the strategies outlined in this book at your disposal, you'll be well on your way to generating novel business ideas and creating engaging content that propels your venture to new heights.

Chapter 1. Understanding ChatGPT and the "Make Money" Niche

Brief Overview of ChatGPT

OpenAI's ChatGPT is not your average AI language model. ChatGPT, short for "Chatbot Generative Pre-trained Transformer," utilizes the latest cutting-edge technology and is based on the advanced GPT-4 architecture. Thanks to this architecture, ChatGPT is a master at understanding and generating text that closely resembles human language, making it a highly valuable tool for various applications.

At the core of ChatGPT is the revolutionary Transformer architecture, a deep learning model that has transformed the field of natural language processing (NLP). By utilizing self-attention mechanisms, the Transformer model can analyze and process text, accurately capturing the nuances and context between words in a given sentence or passage. This allows ChatGPT to generate coherent, contextually relevant, and grammatically correct text that is incredibly human-like, all thanks to its advanced approach to NLP.

To train ChatGPT, a massive amount of text data is fed into the model from different sources, including books, articles, and websites. By analyzing patterns and relationships between words during the training process, the model can gradually learn how to predict the next word in a sentence, and as a result, improve its understanding of language structure, grammar, and context.

One of ChatGPT's greatest advantages is its adaptability, which allows the model to be fine-tuned for specific tasks or domains, making it a highly versatile tool applicable to various applications. From content generation and summarization to question-answering and conversational AI, ChatGPT has the potential to revolutionize the way businesses and individuals interact with and utilize AI technology.

Additionally, ChatGPT's ability to generate high-quality text in a conversational tone makes it an ideal choice for a chat interface. Interacting with ChatGPT through a chat interface is much more intuitive and accessible, requiring little or no API integration or programming knowledge.

While ChatGPT is undoubtedly powerful, it is important to recognize that it, like any AI model, has its limitations. For instance, ChatGPT may produce text that seems plausible but is actually factually incorrect, or it may be sensitive to input phrasing, producing different responses based on minor wording changes. Moreover, ChatGPT may occasionally generate repetitive or verbose outputs, or outputs that are biased in some way. Therefore, it is important to approach the use of ChatGPT with care, and to combine its outputs with human expertise and judgment for optimal results.

Nevertheless, ChatGPT has a wide range of potential applications that extend far beyond content generation. Its abilities in idea generation, brainstorming, and problem-solving make it an invaluable resource for businesses and individuals seeking to excel in their respective domains.

For entrepreneurs, marketers, and freelancers operating in the "make money" niche, ChatGPT can be a game-changer. By leveraging the power of this AI language model, users can unlock new opportunities, generate unique ideas, and create compelling content that drives success in their ventures. The chapters that follow will explore various ways in which ChatGPT can be used to thrive in the "make money" niche, providing strategies, techniques, and examples to help readers make the most of this revolutionary technology.

Overview of the "Make Money" Niche

The "make money" niche is an ever-evolving space that encompasses a plethora of opportunities for individuals seeking to make a fortune. With the advent of advanced technology and the widespread availability of the internet, this niche has grown substantially, presenting numerous avenues for generating income. This section provides a comprehensive overview of the "make money" niche, examining its various facets and illuminating the potential ChatGPT applications in this dynamic arena.

Online entrepreneurship is a burgeoning field within the "make money" niche. Many individuals are taking advantage of the digital landscape to create, market, and sell their products and services. From e-commerce stores and digital products to software development and online courses, the internet has enabled entrepreneurs to reach a global audience with their offerings. ChatGPT is a valuable resource for online entrepreneurs, assisting with concept generation, business plan development, and content creation to drive their success.

Affiliate marketing is another popular method of making money online. In this business model, individuals promote products or services from various companies or platforms and earn a commission for each sale they generate. ChatGPT can assist affiliate marketers in developing compelling content, persuasive product reviews, and effective marketing strategies that resonate with their target audience, thereby helping them to stand out in a crowded and competitive market.

Blogging and content creation are particularly critical for businesses and individuals looking to establish a robust online presence. ChatGPT's ability to generate unique and high-quality content ideas, write engaging blog posts, and create compelling social media updates can help bloggers and content creators to drive traffic to their website and boost their online visibility.

Freelancing is a rapidly growing sector of the "make money" niche, with individuals using their skills and expertise to offer their services to clients worldwide. ChatGPT can assist freelancers in developing new project ideas, creating effective proposals, and improving their service offerings to attract more clients and grow their business.

Investment strategies, including stock market trading, cryptocurrency investing, and real estate, are also significant aspects of the "make money" niche. ChatGPT can provide valuable insights and analysis to help users make informed decisions, as well as generating informative content and investment guides.

Finally, the pursuit of passive income streams is an ever-popular aspect of the "make money" niche, with many people looking to generate income with minimal ongoing effort. Rental properties, dividend stocks, and automated online businesses are all potential sources of passive income. ChatGPT can assist users in identifying and exploring passive income opportunities, as well as creating content to educate others about these methods.

Personal finance and cash management: In the "earn money" sphere, knowing your finances and money management skills are key. ChatGPT can be put to work making informative content on personal finance stuff like budgeting, saving, and investing, helping folks take control of their financial destiny.

Dropshipping and print-on-demand? Those are popular e-commerce models that let enterprising people sell items without worrying about inventory or handling logistics. ChatGPT can lend a hand to these business folks by crafting attention-grabbing product descriptions, efficient email campaigns, and focused social media content to showcase their offerings and boost sales.

As shown by this summary, the "make money" niche is really diverse and offers plenty of opportunities for people to earn income using various techniques and business models. ChatGPT boasts a bunch of potential applications in this area, with the AI tool ready to help users with brainstorming ideas, creating content, and developing strategies. By tapping into the strength of ChatGPT, those in the "make money" niche can discover fresh opportunities, innovate, and propel their ventures to success.

Identifying Opportunities

In today's vast and ever-changing landscape of the "make money" niche, recognizing and seizing opportunities is critical for success. Employing various techniques to identify and capitalize on profitable niches can be challenging, but with the help of ChatGPT, users can streamline their efforts and increase their chances of success. This section explores different methods for identifying opportunities and how ChatGPT can assist in the process.

Thorough market research is crucial for identifying profitable opportunities in the "make money" niche. By analyzing market trends, consumer behavior, and competition, individuals can uncover market gaps that present potential business ideas. ChatGPT can assist in generating market research questions, creating surveys, and analyzing data to uncover insights and identify trends that may lead to promising opportunities.

Keyword research is another useful technique for identifying topics and niches with high demand but low competition. By analyzing search volume, competition, and user intent, individuals can identify lucrative niches and create targeted content that appeals to their audience. ChatGPT can help with keyword research by recommending relevant keywords, generating content ideas based on popular search queries, and advising on SEO strategies to improve online visibility.

Brainstorming sessions with ChatGPT can also be effective for generating new ideas and identifying potential opportunities. By asking questions and receiving suggestions for potential business ideas, content topics, or marketing strategies, users can uncover novel opportunities that were previously overlooked. ChatGPT's ability to think outside the box and provide unique insights can be a valuable asset in this process.

Social listening is another technique that entails monitoring online conversations, social media platforms, and forums to better understand your target audience's needs, preferences, and pain points. ChatGPT can be used to generate questions for social listening, analyze the collected data, and provide insights that can assist users in identifying promising opportunities.

Analyzing competitors' strategies, strengths, and weaknesses can also provide valuable insights into potential opportunities. By evaluating competitors' products, services, and content, users can identify areas where they can differentiate themselves and capitalize on untapped market segments. ChatGPT can be used to develop competitor analysis frameworks, generate ideas for differentiation, and provide guidance on developing unique value propositions.

Networking and collaboration can also lead to new ideas, partnerships, and opportunities in the "make money" niche. ChatGPT can assist users in creating compelling pitches for potential collaborators or investors by generating conversation starters and recommending networking strategies.

Finally, users can leverage their own personal skills, interests, and experiences to identify potential business ideas or content topics that align with their expertise and personal brand. ChatGPT can suggest potential business ideas based on user inputs about their skills and interests and provide guidance on how to successfully leverage personal strengths in the "make money" niche.

By employing these techniques and leveraging the power of ChatGPT, users can effectively identify and capitalize on opportunities in the "make money" niche. With ChatGPT's unique insights, innovative ideas, and assistance in developing effective strategies, users can stay ahead of the competition and maximize their earning potential in this ever-changing landscape.

Examples of ChatGPT's potential impact on the niche

ChatGPT's impact on the "make money" niche is vast and wide-ranging, spanning across various business models, content creation methods, and marketing strategies. With its incredible capabilities, ChatGPT offers individuals in this niche the opportunity to unlock new and exciting opportunities, optimize their efforts, and ultimately drive success in their ventures. In this section, we'll delve deeper into some specific examples of how ChatGPT can make a significant impact on the "make money" niche.

For affiliate marketers, creating compelling content that can effectively promote products or services can be a significant challenge. However, with ChatGPT, individuals can create high-quality product reviews, comparisons, and promotional content that resonate with their target audience and boost conversion rates. By utilizing ChatGPT's content generation capabilities, affiliate marketers can streamline their content creation process and increase the effectiveness of their marketing campaigns.

Writing persuasive product descriptions for e-commerce is another time-consuming task that can hinder entrepreneurs' efforts to drive sales and foster customer trust. With ChatGPT, individuals can create powerful product descriptions that highlight each item's unique features and benefits, which can help attract more customers and increase revenue.

Financial content creation is another area where ChatGPT can be a valuable resource. The AI model can generate informative and engaging articles, guides, and analyses on a wide range of financial topics, including stock market trends, cryptocurrency investment strategies, and budgeting advice. By leveraging ChatGPT's ability to create high-quality financial content, individuals can establish themselves as authorities in their niche and attract a loyal audience.

Generating ideas for passive income streams requires creative thinking and the ability to spot untapped opportunities. With ChatGPT, individuals can generate ideas for potential passive income streams such as niche websites, e-books, and online courses. By utilizing ChatGPT's creative thinking capabilities, individuals can discover unique passive income opportunities that align with their skills, interests, and market demand.

In the "make money" niche, having a strong social media presence is essential for connecting with the target audience, sharing valuable content, and promoting products or services. ChatGPT can be used to create engaging social media posts, captions, and updates that drive follower engagement and interaction, helping users grow their online presence and reach.

These examples are just a few of the many ways ChatGPT can positively impact the "make money" niche. By leveraging ChatGPT's incredible capabilities, individuals can optimize their content creation, marketing, and idea generation efforts, leading to greater success and profitability in their chosen ventures.

Chapter 2. Brainstorming Business Ideas with ChatGPT

Techniques for Brainstorming

Brainstorming is a crucial step in cooking up fresh business ideas and spotting potential opportunities in the "make money" domain. ChatGPT's prowess can be harnessed to spark brainstorming sessions that yield one-of-a-kind, captivating concepts. In this section, we'll examine various brainstorming techniques that can be paired with ChatGPT to amp up the idea generation process.

1. Mind mapping is a visual tactic that aids folks in organizing and structuring their thoughts around a core concept. Users can craft a mind map with ChatGPT by supplying a central theme or subject, and the AI will churn out related ideas, subtopics, and links. This approach lets users probe multiple facets of a notion and reveal hidden gems.
Prompt example: "Create a mind map for an online course in the 'make money' niche with related subtopics and ideas."

2. The SCAMPER technique is an acronym that embodies Substitute, Combine, Adapt, Modify, Put to another use, Eliminate, and Reverse. This method involves posing a series of questions that encourage users to ponder their idea from various angles and pinpoint potential enhancements or tweaks. ChatGPT can cook up SCAMPER questions and suggest possible alterations to an idea, helping users polish their concepts and think more imaginatively.
Prompt example: "Using the SCAMPER method, suggest ways to improve and innovate an online course on affiliate marketing."

3. The 5 Whys tactic involves asking "why" repeatedly (usually five times) to dig up the root cause of a problem or to dive deeper into a specific idea. Users can utilize ChatGPT to carry out a 5 Whys exercise, posing

queries and receiving responses that help them explore the underlying motives, implications, or challenges of their business notions.

Prompt example: "I want to create an online course about passive income. Why is this a good idea?"

4. Rolestorming is a brainstorming method where individuals take on different roles or personas to generate ideas from various viewpoints. ChatGPT can be a handy tool for rolestorming since users can direct the AI to assume different roles (e.g., customer, investor, competitor) and provide insights or suggestions from those perspectives. This technique can assist users in better grasping their target audience's needs and preferences while also spotting potential opportunities or hurdles that were previously hidden.

   Prompt example: "Imagine you are a customer looking for an online course in the 'make money' niche. What topics would you be most interested in learning about?"

5. Random Word Association: In this approach, random words are produced and used as a springboard to generate new ideas or connections. ChatGPT can be employed to create random words, phrases, or concepts and then suggest how these seemingly unrelated terms can be linked to the central business idea. This method spurs users to think outside the box to unearth novel connections or concepts.

   Prompt example: "Generate a random word and suggest a connection between that word and an online course in the 'make money' niche."

6. Forced Connections: Forced connections is a technique where folks blend two or more unrelated notions to find a connection or generate a new idea. ChatGPT can be used to concoct seemingly unrelated ideas and help users connect them, resulting in groundbreaking business concepts or inventive solutions to problems.

   Prompt example: "Combine 'cryptocurrency' and 'cooking' to create a unique idea for an online course in the 'make money' niche."

7. The Six Thinking Hats method, conceived by Edward de Bono, entails examining a problem or idea from six distinct angles, symbolized by various "hats," which include: White Hat (facts and info), Red Hat (emotions and intuition), Black Hat (risks and challenges), Yellow Hat (benefits and opportunities), Green Hat (creativity and alternatives), and Blue Hat (process and organization). Users can gain a more well-rounded understanding of their ideas and pinpoint potential opportunities, challenges, and enhancements by instructing ChatGPT to adopt each of these perspectives in turn.
Prompt example: "Using the Six Thinking Hats method, evaluate the idea of creating an online course about dropshipping in the 'make money' niche."

8. SWOT Analysis: SWOT analysis is a strategic planning instrument that identifies a business idea's or venture's strengths, weaknesses, opportunities, and threats. ChatGPT can perform a SWOT analysis, offering insights and recommendations for each of the four categories. This method assists users in evaluating the feasibility of their ideas and pinpointing potential areas for improvement or growth. By understanding the strengths and weaknesses of their ideas, as well as the opportunities and threats they may encounter, users can make well-informed decisions about whether to pursue a particular venture and develop strategies to overcome potential challenges.
Prompt example: "Conduct a SWOT analysis for an online course on personal finance and investing in the 'make money' niche."

By employing these brainstorming techniques in tandem with ChatGPT, users can enhance their creative thinking and generate a wealth of inventive business ideas in the "make money" domain. Individuals can unearth unique opportunities, refine concepts, and develop a deeper comprehension of their target market and competitive landscape by experimenting with different methods and blending them as necessary. Users can optimize their idea generation endeavors and lay the groundwork for success in their chosen ventures by leveraging the power of ChatGPT in the brainstorming process.

Developing Innovative Offerings

The capacity to generate innovative offerings is crucial for success in the "make money" niche. Crafting products, services, or content that stand out can help you distinguish your business from competitors and better address the needs of your target audience. In this section, we will explore approaches for creating innovative offerings with the help of ChatGPT.

1. Customer-centric design: A customer-focused approach involves designing your offerings based on your target audience's preferences, needs, and challenges. ChatGPT can assist you in gathering information about your target market by generating questions for customer interviews, creating user personas, or pinpointing potential customer needs that your offerings could satisfy. By concentrating on their requirements, you can create products, services, or content that truly resonate with your audience.
Prompt example: "Generate interview questions to better understand the needs and preferences of potential clients for a freelance writing service."

2. Divergent thinking involves generating a wide variety of ideas, even if they seem unconventional or unrelated to the issue at hand. ChatGPT can be used to encourage divergent thinking by providing numerous creative ideas, helping you explore fresh perspectives, and discovering untapped opportunities. Once you have generated a diverse range of ideas, you can employ convergent thinking to choose the most promising concepts and refine them into actionable offerings.
Prompt example: "Provide a list of unconventional ideas for services or features that a freelance writing business could offer to stand out in the 'make money' niche."

3. Iterative development involves creating a prototype or early version of your offering, testing it, gathering feedback, and making improvements based on that feedback. This cycle of prototyping, testing, and refining continues until the offering achieves the desired level of quality and effectiveness. ChatGPT can help with iterative development by

generating prototype ideas, suggesting improvements based on user feedback, and advising you on refining your offerings to better meet the needs of your target audience.

Prompt example: "Suggest a prototype for a unique feature in a freelance writing platform, and provide guidance on testing and refining the feature based on user feedback."

4. Cross-pollination involves borrowing ideas, concepts, or techniques from one industry or field and applying them to another. ChatGPT can be used to generate cross-pollination ideas by helping you identify trends, technologies, or strategies from other industries that can be adapted to create innovative offerings in the "make money" niche. By combining ideas from various sources, you can create distinctive products, services, or content that sets your business apart from competitors.

Prompt example: "Identify a trend, technology, or strategy from another industry that could be adapted to create an innovative offering for a freelance writing business in the 'make money' niche."

5. Experimentation entails trying new approaches, technologies, or methods to develop innovative offerings. ChatGPT can be used to generate experiment ideas, suggest potential technologies or methods to explore, and even provide guidance on how to design and execute effective experiments. By adopting an experimental mindset, you can continuously innovate and enhance your offerings, ensuring your business remains competitive in the ever-evolving "make money" niche.

Prompt example: "Propose an experiment to test a new approach or technology for improving the client experience in a freelance writing service."

6. Cooperation and team spirit: Joining forces with others can spark the birth of fresh ideas and solutions that might have been impossible when working solo. ChatGPT can grease the wheels of collaboration by whipping up conversation starters, recommending teamwork tools or platforms, and offering guidance on how to effectively manage and

orchestrate team efforts. By tapping into the collective expertise and imagination of a diverse bunch of individuals, you can create more inventive and efficient offerings.

Prompt example: "Generate conversation starters and suggest collaboration tools for a remote team working on a freelance writing platform to encourage creative problem-solving and innovation."

7. Failure can be a treasure trove of learning and motivation when it comes to crafting innovative offerings. By scrutinizing past failures and grasping the factors that contributed to them, you can pinpoint areas needing improvement and devise strategies to sidestep similar snags in the future. ChatGPT can be employed to extract insights from previous flops, propose potential lessons learned, and provide direction on how to apply those lessons to future endeavors.

Prompt example: "Analyze a past failure in the freelance writing industry and suggest potential lessons learned that can be applied to a new business venture in the 'make money' niche."

By embracing these tactics and harnessing ChatGPT's abilities, you can forge innovative offerings that set your company apart in the "make money" niche while also catering to the evolving needs of your target audience. Concentrating on constant improvement, experimentation, and a customer-centric mindset will ensure that your products, services, and content stay relevant and effective in this competitive arena. Adopting an innovative attitude and adapting to the ever-shifting market dynamics can differentiate your company, cultivate a loyal customer following, and fuel long-term growth and success in the "make money" niche. ChatGPT, with its vast knowledge and knack for generating imaginative ideas, can be an invaluable ally in your pursuit to develop cutting-edge offerings that resonate with your audience and help you stand out in a bustling market.

Validating and refining ideas

Once you've assembled a roster of potential business ideas and offerings, it's crucial to validate and refine them to make sure they're practical in the "make money" niche. In this section, we will delve into tactics for validating and refining your ideas using ChatGPT.

1. Market research aids you in grasping the competitive landscape, gauging market demand, and pinpointing trends or opportunities that could impact your offerings. ChatGPT can be employed to concoct survey or interview questions, propose secondary research sources, or analyze and condense data to help you make well-informed decisions about your ideas.
Prompt example: "Generate questions for a survey to assess the demand for a personal finance coaching service in the 'make money' niche."

2. Gathering feedback from prospective or current customers is a priceless way to validate and polish your ideas. ChatGPT can support you in crafting surveys or questionnaires, whipping up prompts for focus groups, and dissecting feedback to spot common themes, concerns, or suggestions. By integrating customer feedback, you can ensure that your offerings resonate with your target audience and effectively address their needs.
Prompt example: "Create a questionnaire to gather feedback from potential clients about the most valuable features they would like to see in a personal finance coaching service."

3. Hypothesis testing involves creating a testable prediction about the outcome of a particular change or feature and amassing data to see if the prediction holds true. ChatGPT can be utilized to generate hypotheses, design experiments or tests, and scrutinize the results to determine if your idea or offering is on the right path or requires further refinement.
Prompt example: "Develop a hypothesis and design an experiment to test the effectiveness of offering one-on-one video consultations as part of a personal finance coaching service."

4. Minimum Viable Product (MVP): An MVP is a stripped-down version of your offering that contains only the most essential features or elements, allowing you to examine its market viability and gather feedback for future development. ChatGPT can help you pinpoint the core components of your MVP, suggest testing and validation approaches, and offer guidance on refining your offering based on feedback received.

    Prompt example: "Identify the core components of an MVP for a personal finance coaching service and suggest strategies for testing and validation."

5. Financial projections and analysis: Appraising the financial feasibility of your ideas is vital for determining their potential for success. ChatGPT can assist you in crafting financial projections, estimating costs and revenue, and carrying out a break-even analysis to gauge the profitability of your offerings. This information can aid you in making informed decisions about whether to pursue a specific idea or adjust your strategy to enhance its financial prospects.

    Prompt example: "Help me create financial projections for a personal finance coaching service, including estimated costs, revenue, and break-even point."

6. Risk assessment: It's essential to identify and evaluate the risks linked to your ideas in order to devise contingency plans and mitigate potential hurdles. ChatGPT can support you in conducting a risk assessment by producing a list of potential risks, recommending strategies for handling or mitigating them, and advising you on crafting contingency plans to ensure your business's resilience.

    Prompt example: "Generate a list of potential risks associated with launching a personal finance coaching service and suggest strategies for managing or mitigating those risks."

7. Continuous improvement: As markets evolve and customer needs shift, the process of validating and refining your ideas should be persistent. ChatGPT can be employed to keep tabs on trends, gather feedback, and propose enhancements to your offerings, ensuring their relevance and effectiveness in the ever-changing "make money" niche.
Prompt example: "Provide guidance on how to stay updated on industry trends and best practices in the personal finance niche, and suggest ways to apply this knowledge to continuously improve a personal finance coaching service."

Real world examples and case studies

In this section, we'll explore genuine examples and case studies of how businesses in the "make money" niche have harnessed ChatGPT to develop and enhance their offerings. These instances can act as motivation and inspiration for your own entrepreneurial endeavors. A prompt is furnished for each example to illustrate how ChatGPT can be employed for similar purposes.

1. Crafting an Online Course. A content creator in the "make money" niche tapped into ChatGPT to generate ideas and fashion an online course on passive income strategies. ChatGPT contributed to shaping the course structure, devising engaging content, and even whipping up marketing materials.
Prompt example: "Outline a comprehensive online course on passive income strategies, including module topics, learning objectives, and key takeaways for each module."

2. Blogging about Affiliate Marketing. An affiliate marketer utilized ChatGPT to research and pen high-quality blog posts on various "make money" topics, enabling them to rank higher in search engine results and boost affiliate sales.
Prompt example: "Write an informative and engaging blog post on the top 5 affiliate marketing strategies for beginners in the 'make money' niche."

3. Financial Coaching Services. ChatGPT was harnessed by a financial coach to create a distinctive value proposition for their coaching services, which centered on helping individuals in the "make money" niche attain financial independence. ChatGPT also aided clients in crafting personalized coaching plans tailored to their specific needs and goals.
Prompt example: "Create a unique value proposition for a financial coaching service targeting individuals in the 'make money' niche and suggest personalized coaching plans for three different client profiles."

4. Online Store. An entrepreneur employed ChatGPT to generate and validate product ideas for an e-commerce store in the "make money" niche, concentrating on selling digital products and tools to support customers in building and expanding their online ventures.
Prompt example: "Generate a list of digital product ideas for an e-commerce store in the 'make money' niche and provide a brief analysis of the market demand and competition for each idea."

5. Social Media Marketing Agency. ChatGPT was utilized by a social media marketing agency to conceive creative campaign ideas for clients in the "make money" niche, allowing them to stand out from the competition and achieve improved results with their advertising endeavors.
Prompt example: "Develop three creative social media marketing campaign ideas for a client in the 'make money' niche, including target audience, goals, key messaging, and recommended platforms."

These real-world instances and case studies exhibit ChatGPT's adaptability and potential in aiding businesses in the "make money" niche. You can employ ChatGPT's capabilities to develop, refine, and grow your own venture in this competitive market by using the supplied prompts or tailoring them to your specific needs.

Chapter 3. Crafting Business Plans and Strategies with ChatGPT

Creating business plans

A robust business plan lays the groundwork for any thriving venture in the "make money" niche. ChatGPT can be an invaluable asset in crafting a comprehensive, well-researched, and actionable business plan that tackles all crucial aspects of your venture. In this section, we'll discuss how ChatGPT can support you in devising business plans, encompassing the following elements:

1. Executive Summary: The executive summary encapsulates your company's mission, vision, objectives, and key selling points. ChatGPT can help you forge a concise yet potent executive summary that captures the essence of your company and its potential for triumph.
   Prompt example: "Write an executive summary for a business in the 'make money' niche that focuses on offering a platform for freelancers to sell their digital products and services."

2. Company Description: This section delves into your company's details, such as its legal structure, history, and core values. ChatGPT can aid you in creating an exhaustive company description that underscores your company's unique attributes and positions it for success.
   Prompt example: "Provide a detailed company description for an e-commerce store in the 'make money' niche specializing in digital products for online entrepreneurs."

3. A comprehensive market analysis will help you grasp the competitive landscape, target audience, and market opportunities. ChatGPT can support you in generating market research questions, locating relevant data sources, and synthesizing data to inform your business strategy.
   Prompt example: "Conduct a market analysis for a financial coaching service targeting individuals in the 'make money' niche, including information on the target audience, competition, and market opportunities."

4. Products and Services: In this section, you'll outline the products and services your company offers, emphasizing their unique features and benefits. ChatGPT can assist you in fashioning compelling descriptions of your offerings as well as pinpointing ways to differentiate them from competitors.
Prompt example: "Describe the products and services offered by a membership site in the 'make money' niche focused on providing exclusive access to expert advice, resources, and tools for growing online businesses."

5. Marketing and Sales Strategy: Engaging your target audience and driving revenue necessitates a well-defined marketing and sales strategy. ChatGPT can help in devising marketing plans, identifying ideal sales channels, and conceiving promotional campaign ideas.
Prompt example: "Create a marketing and sales strategy for a SaaS business in the 'make money' niche offering an all-in-one platform for managing and growing affiliate marketing campaigns."

6. The operational plan sketches out the day-to-day activities needed to operate your business, such as management, staffing, logistics, and technology. ChatGPT can aid you in creating an efficient operational plan that caters to your company's needs and ensures seamless workflow.
Prompt example: "Develop an operational plan for an online course platform in the 'make money' niche, including details on management, staffing, logistics, and technology requirements."

7. Financial Projections: Financial projections help you estimate your company's costs, revenue, and profitability. ChatGPT can assist with financial forecasting, break-even analysis, and pinpointing potential risks or challenges.
Prompt example: "Prepare financial projections for a content creation agency in the 'make money' niche, including estimated costs, revenue, profitability, and break-even analysis."

By harnessing ChatGPT's capabilities, you can construct a comprehensive and well-researched business plan that will serve as the backbone for your venture in the "make money" niche. This sturdy foundation will help you navigate the competitive landscape, make informed decisions, and achieve long-term success.

Developing marketing strategies

For businesses in the "make money" niche, reaching their target audience and driving revenue necessitates a well-designed marketing strategy. ChatGPT can be a valuable asset for devising effective, innovative, and customized marketing strategies tailored to your specific business needs. In this section, we'll explore various aspects of marketing strategy development, such as:

1. Identifying Your Target Audience: Understanding who your target audience is essential for crafting marketing campaigns that resonate with them. ChatGPT can support you in pinpointing your target audience's demographics, psychographics, and pain points.
Prompt example: "Define the target audience for a financial coaching service in the 'make money' niche, including demographic and psychographic characteristics, as well as common pain points."

2. Setting Marketing Objectives: Establishing clear marketing objectives steers and gauges the success of your strategy. ChatGPT can help you devise SMART (Specific, Measurable, Achievable, Relevant, and Time-bound) marketing objectives.
Prompt example: "Create three SMART marketing objectives for a membership site in the 'make money' niche focused on providing exclusive access to expert advice, resources, and tools for growing online businesses."

3. Choosing Marketing Channels: Selecting the appropriate marketing channels can help you reach your target audience effectively and efficiently. ChatGPT can aid you in determining the best channels for

your company, such as social media, email, content marketing, and paid advertising.
Prompt example: "Identify the most effective marketing channels for promoting a SaaS business in the 'make money' niche offering an all-in-one platform for managing and growing affiliate marketing campaigns."

4. Creating a Unique Selling Proposition (USP): A robust USP sets your company apart from the competition and highlights the unique value it offers. ChatGPT can help you develop a compelling USP that will resonate with your target audience.
Prompt example: "Develop a unique selling proposition for an e-commerce store in the 'make money' niche specializing in digital products for online entrepreneurs."

5. Content Marketing Strategy: Producing high-quality, relevant content can help your company build trust, establish authority, and drive organic traffic. ChatGPT can support you in generating content ideas, creating engaging content, and optimizing it for search engines.
Prompt example: "Outline a content marketing strategy for an affiliate marketing blog in the 'make money' niche, including content topics, formats, and SEO best practices."

6. Social media platforms present valuable opportunities to connect with your target audience, elevate brand awareness, and encourage engagement. ChatGPT can assist you in formulating creative social media campaigns, determining optimal posting schedules, and engaging with your audience effectively.
Prompt example: "Design a social media marketing campaign for a personal finance coaching service in the 'make money' niche, including platform selection, content ideas, and posting frequency."

7. Email Marketing: One of the most potent ways to nurture leads, foster customer loyalty, and drive sales is through email marketing. ChatGPT

can aid in crafting compelling email campaigns, developing targeted email sequences, and optimizing deliverability and open rates.

Prompt example: "Create an email marketing strategy for an online course platform in the 'make money' niche, including lead magnet ideas, email sequence structure, and best practices for subject lines and content."

8. Monitoring and analyzing your marketing efforts can help you optimize performance, identify areas for improvement, and make data-driven decisions. ChatGPT can support you in determining key performance indicators (KPIs) and implementing analytics tools to track the success of your marketing endeavors.

Prompt example: "Identify the key performance indicators (KPIs) for measuring the success of a content creation agency's marketing strategy in the 'make money' niche and suggest analytics tools to track these metrics."

By leveraging ChatGPT's capabilities, you can develop a comprehensive and tailored marketing strategy that effectively reaches your target audience and drives revenue in the "make money" niche. ChatGPT can help you at every stage of the marketing process, from identifying the right marketing channels to crafting a compelling unique selling proposition. We can support you in creating innovative campaigns and making data-driven decisions. By continuously monitoring your marketing efforts and analyzing performance metrics, you can optimize your strategy for long-term success and growth in this competitive market.

Analyzing competitors

Grasping your competition is vital for businesses in the "make money" niche to stand out and stay ahead. ChatGPT can be a valuable ally for conducting in-depth competitor analysis and spotting opportunities for growth and enhancement. In this section, we'll discuss various facets of competitor analysis, such as:

1. Identifying Key Competitors: The first step in competitor analysis is pinpointing your niche's primary rivals. Based on your specific offerings and target audience, ChatGPT can help you compile a list of direct and indirect competitors.
   Prompt example: "Identify the key competitors for an online course platform in the 'make money' niche, focused on teaching passive income strategies."

2. Analyzing Competitor Offerings: A thorough understanding of your competitors' products and services can help you spot gaps and differentiation opportunities in your offerings. ChatGPT can assist with competitor research and evaluation, including their unique features, benefits, and pricing structures.
   Prompt example: "Analyze the product offerings, unique features, benefits, and pricing structures of the top three competitors for a SaaS business in the 'make money' niche, offering an all-in-one platform for managing and growing affiliate marketing campaigns."

3. Examining Competitors' Marketing Strategies: Looking into your competitors' marketing strategies can uncover information about their target audience, messaging, and tactics. ChatGPT can aid you in evaluating their marketing efforts, such as content marketing, social media marketing, and paid advertising campaigns.
   Prompt example: "Assess the marketing strategies of three competitors for a financial coaching service in the 'make money' niche, focusing on their content marketing, social media, and paid advertising efforts."

4. Evaluating Competitor Strengths and Weaknesses: A thorough examination of your competitors' strengths and weaknesses can help you pinpoint areas where your company can excel and areas where it needs to improve. ChatGPT can support you in conducting a SWOT analysis of your competitors' strengths, weaknesses, opportunities, and threats.

Prompt example: "Conduct a SWOT analysis for the top three competitors of an e-commerce store in the 'make money' niche, specializing in digital products for online entrepreneurs."

5. Customer reviews and testimonials from competitors can offer valuable insights into their strengths and weaknesses, as well as possible opportunities. ChatGPT can assist you in identifying key themes and trends in customer feedback to inform your business strategy.
Prompt example: "Analyze customer reviews and testimonials for three competitors of a membership site in the 'make money' niche, focused on providing exclusive access to expert advice, resources, and tools for growing online businesses. Identify key themes and trends from the feedback."

6. Benchmarking Key Performance Indicators (KPIs): Comparing your company's performance to that of its competitors can aid you in recognizing areas for improvement and setting ambitious yet achievable goals. ChatGPT can help you select relevant KPIs and compare your performance to industry standards.
Prompt example: "Identify relevant key performance indicators (KPIs) for a content creation agency in the 'make money' niche and suggest industry benchmarks for comparison."

7. Identifying Competitive Advantages and Opportunities: Using your competitor analysis, you can discern your company's competitive advantages and growth opportunities. ChatGPT can help you synthesize your findings and develop a strategy to capitalize on your strengths while addressing your weaknesses.
Prompt example: "Based on the competitor analysis for a personal finance coaching service in the 'make money' niche, identify competitive advantages and opportunities for growth, as well as strategies for addressing weaknesses."

By utilizing ChatGPT's capabilities, you can conduct comprehensive competitor analysis, which will help you stay ahead in the competitive "make money" niche. By carefully examining your competitors' offerings, marketing strategies, customer feedback, and performance metrics, you can pinpoint areas where your company can excel and areas where it needs to improve. By leveraging these insights, you can capitalize on your competitive advantages, address your weaknesses, and ultimately create a more successful and sustainable business in the "make money" niche. Utilizing ChatGPT's powerful capabilities, you can stay informed and adapt to the ever-changing market dynamics, ensuring long-term growth and success. Embrace a thorough understanding of your competitors to navigate the competitive landscape and build a more resilient business in the "make money" niche.

Examples of successful strategies

In this section, we'll explore several real-world examples of flourishing strategies in the "make money" niche, showcasing how businesses have creatively employed ChatGPT to enhance their offerings, marketing initiatives, and overall performance.

1. Online Course Platform: ChatGPT was utilized by a renowned online course platform in the "make money" niche to craft a unique selling proposition (USP) that accentuated its personalized learning experience, expert instructors, and success-driven community. The platform deployed ChatGPT to generate captivating, SEO-optimized content that attracted organic traffic, positioning itself as a trusted authority in the niche. By adopting data-driven marketing tactics, the platform optimized its email marketing campaigns, resulting in elevated open rates and conversions. Consequently, the platform witnessed a substantial increase in course enrollment and revenue.
Prompt example: "Generate a unique selling proposition (USP) for an online course platform in the 'make money' niche, focusing on personalized learning experience, expert instructors, and a success-driven community."

2. Affiliate Marketing Blog: An affiliate marketing blog in the "make money" niche employed ChatGPT to produce high-quality content ideas that resonated with its target audience. The blog used ChatGPT to generate well-researched, long-form articles brimming with actionable tips and strategies for affiliate marketers. Additionally, the blog utilized ChatGPT to create engaging social media content and cultivate an active, loyal community. By concentrating on delivering valuable content and establishing itself as a reliable resource, the blog experienced a surge in organic traffic and affiliate income.
Prompt example: "Suggest five high-quality, long-form content ideas for an affiliate marketing blog in the 'make money' niche that provide actionable tips and strategies for readers."

3. Financial Coaching Service: ChatGPT was harnessed by a financial coaching service in the "make money" niche to scrutinize its competitors' marketing strategies and pinpoint opportunities for differentiation. Based on the insights gathered, the service devised a targeted marketing campaign aimed at addressing the specific pain points of its target audience. The service also utilized ChatGPT to create personalized email sequences that nurtured leads and promoted conversions. As a result, the coaching service enjoyed an influx of new clients and a higher rate of client retention.
Prompt example: "Analyze the marketing strategies of three competitors for a financial coaching service in the 'make money' niche and suggest ways to differentiate the service and target unique pain points of the audience."

4. Digital Goods E-commerce Site: An e-commerce store specializing in digital products for online entrepreneurs in the "make money" niche turned to ChatGPT to craft engaging product descriptions that emphasized the unique features and benefits of its offerings. The store utilized ChatGPT to develop a data-driven marketing strategy that incorporated targeted social media advertising and email marketing campaigns, which directly addressed the needs and desires of its target

audience. This approach led to a notable increase in sales, customer satisfaction, and repeat purchases.

Prompt example: "Write a compelling product description for a digital product in the 'make money' niche that highlights its unique features and benefits for online entrepreneurs."

5. SaaS Company for Affiliate Marketing Campaigns: A SaaS company in the "make money" niche employed ChatGPT to determine the most effective marketing channels for promoting its all-in-one platform for managing and growing affiliate marketing campaigns. ChatGPT generated engaging content for the company's blog, social media, and email marketing campaigns, educating prospects on the benefits of its platform and the opportunities it offered to affiliate marketers. As a result, user acquisition, customer retention, and overall revenue rose in the SaaS sector.

Prompt example: "Identify the most effective marketing channels for promoting a SaaS business in the 'make money' niche that offers an all-in-one platform for managing and growing affiliate marketing campaigns."

These examples demonstrate how businesses in the "make money" niche can effectively leverage ChatGPT to develop innovative offerings, potent marketing strategies, and competitive analysis. By capitalizing on ChatGPT's capabilities, businesses can adapt to the ever-evolving market landscape and secure long-term success in this highly competitive niche.

Chapter 4. Content Creation with ChatGPT

Utilizing ChatGPT for content types

ChatGPT's versatility makes it a priceless resource for generating an array of content in the "make money" niche. Owing to its capacity to comprehend context, create coherent text, and adapt to specific writing styles, it's a fantastic solution for crafting diverse content that captivates and converts your target audience. In this section, we'll explore several types of content that can be effectively created using ChatGPT, as well as tips for leveraging AI to achieve the best results.

1. ChatGPT can generate well-researched, informative, and engaging long-form content for your blog or website. By providing a topic or specific keywords, you can obtain relevant and valuable content that appeals to your target audience, enhances your online presence, and boosts your search engine rankings.
Prompt example: "Write a 1,500-word blog post on the top 10 passive income strategies in the 'make money' niche, focusing on the benefits and potential risks of each strategy."

2. Social Media Content: Producing engaging and shareable social media content is essential for businesses in the "make money" niche to expand their following and brand awareness. ChatGPT can create posts, captions, and responses for various social media platforms, helping you maintain an active and engaging online presence.
Prompt example: "Generate 10 engaging social media post ideas for an online course platform in the 'make money' niche, focusing on promoting a new course on affiliate marketing strategies."

3. ChatGPT can assist you in crafting video scripts and webinar content that educates, entertains, and inspires your audience. You can use ChatGPT to create well-structured and engaging scripts for YouTube videos, explainer videos, or live webinars that drive conversions and foster trust with your target audience.

Prompt example: "Write a script for a 10-minute YouTube video explaining the basics of dropshipping as a 'make money' strategy for beginners."

4. ChatGPT enables you to develop comprehensive e-books and guides that offer in-depth information on various topics within the "make money" niche. By leveraging the AI's capabilities, you can generate well-organized, insightful, and actionable content that establishes you as an authority in your field and adds value to your audience.
Prompt example: "Outline a 50-page e-book on building and scaling a profitable Amazon FBA business in the 'make money' niche, covering the essentials from product research to marketing and optimization."

5. ChatGPT can help you create compelling case studies and testimonials that showcase the success of your products or services. By using AI to highlight key outcomes, challenges, and solutions, you can craft persuasive narratives that resonate with potential customers and demonstrate the effectiveness of your offerings.
Prompt example: "Write a case study showcasing the success of a client who used a financial coaching service in the 'make money' niche to reduce debt and increase their passive income."

6. ChatGPT can create professional press releases and newsletters that effectively communicate important updates, announcements, or achievements related to your business in the "make money" niche. By providing key information and a newsworthy angle, you can craft content that captures the attention of media outlets, industry influencers, and your target audience.
Prompt example: "Write a press release announcing the launch of a groundbreaking SaaS platform in the 'make money' niche that simplifies and automates the management of affiliate marketing campaigns."

By utilizing ChatGPT for these various content types, businesses in the "make money" niche can generate high-quality, targeted, and engaging content that connects with their audience, improves their online presence, and ultimately drives growth and revenue.

Crafting email campaigns

Email marketing remains a potent tool for "make money" businesses, enabling them to connect with their audience, nurture leads, and drive conversions. ChatGPT can help you craft captivating and effective email campaigns that resonate with your subscribers and encourage them to take action. In this section, we'll discuss various strategies for creating email campaigns using ChatGPT and how to employ AI for optimal results.

1. Welcome Emails: A robust welcome email builds trust and sets the tone for your relationship with new subscribers. ChatGPT can help you develop personalized welcome emails that introduce your brand, emphasize the value you deliver, and lay out expectations for future communications.
Prompt example: "Write a welcome email for new subscribers of a financial coaching service in the 'make money' niche, explaining the benefits of joining and what they can expect to receive."

2. Sharing valuable educational content with your subscribers can help you position yourself as an authority in your niche and foster trust with your audience. ChatGPT can create informative and engaging content on various "make money" topics, assisting you in nurturing leads and cultivating loyal followers.
Prompt example: "Create a three-part email series teaching the fundamentals of affiliate marketing, including choosing profitable niches, selecting affiliate products, and driving targeted traffic."

3. Promotional Campaigns: When promoting a product, service, or event, it's crucial to craft engaging and persuasive emails that highlight the benefits and prompt your subscribers to act. ChatGPT can help you develop promotional campaigns that showcase your unique selling proposition, address potential objections, and drive conversions.

Prompt example: "Write a launch email for an online course in the 'make money' niche, focusing on the benefits of the course, a special limited-time offer, and a strong call to action."

4. Follow-up and Reminder Emails: Keeping your subscribers informed of crucial dates, events, or offers is vital for maintaining engagement and driving conversions. ChatGPT can assist you in creating follow-up and reminder emails that keep your audience informed and motivated to act without coming across as pushy or salesy.
Prompt example: "Craft a reminder email for subscribers who have not yet signed up for a free webinar on passive income strategies in the 'make money' niche, emphasizing the value of attending and the approaching deadline."

5. Re-engagement Campaigns: An essential strategy for maximizing your email list's potential is to reignite the interest of inactive subscribers. ChatGPT can help you develop re-engagement campaigns that remind subscribers of the value you offer, share new and exciting updates, and encourage them to engage with your content and offerings once more.
Prompt example: "Write an email to re-engage inactive subscribers of an affiliate marketing blog in the 'make money' niche, sharing recent high-quality content and inviting them to join an exclusive Facebook group."

6. Testimonials and Success Stories: Sharing testimonials and success stories with your subscribers can help build trust and showcase the efficacy of your products or services. ChatGPT can assist you in crafting persuasive emails that demonstrate the real-world impact of your offerings, creating social proof and spurring potential customers to take action.
Prompt example: "Create an email featuring a success story of a user who achieved financial freedom through an e-commerce store training program in the 'make money' niche, highlighting the key strategies they implemented and the results they achieved."

By leveraging ChatGPT's capabilities to create various types of email campaigns, businesses in the "make money" niche can forge strong relationships with their subscribers, establish trust and authority, and ultimately drive growth and revenue. The AI's ability to generate targeted, engaging, and persuasive content makes it a valuable asset for any email marketing strategy.

Developing sales copy

Sales copy is a crucial element of any profitable "make money" business, as it drives conversions and persuades potential customers to purchase your products or services. ChatGPT can help you craft efficient and captivating sales copy that connects with your target audience and entices them to act. In this section, we'll discuss several strategies for creating sales copy with ChatGPT and how to employ AI for optimal outcomes.

1. Headlines and Subheadlines: Crafting eye-catching headlines and subheadlines is vital for capturing your target audience's interest and persuading them to read further. ChatGPT can help you create headlines that are clear, concise, and alluring, prompting readers to delve deeper into your sales copy.
Prompt example: "Generate 5 different headlines for a sales page promoting an online course on creating and selling digital products in the 'make money' niche."

2. Introduction and Hook: Your sales copy should commence with a strong connection to your audience and a compelling reason for them to keep reading. ChatGPT can help you craft hooks that address the pain points, desires, and goals of your target audience, fostering a sense of urgency and curiosity.
Prompt example: "Write an engaging introduction for a sales page offering a financial coaching service in the 'make money' niche, focusing on the key challenges faced by the target audience and the potential benefits of the service."

3. The unique selling proposition (USP) of your product or service sets it apart from competitors and showcases its value to your target audience. ChatGPT can assist you in creating a clear and persuasive USP that emphasizes your offering's distinct features and benefits, boosting perceived value and driving conversions.
Prompt example: "Craft a unique selling proposition for a SaaS platform that simplifies and automates the management of affiliate marketing campaigns in the 'make money' niche, emphasizing its unique features and advantages."

4. Features and Benefits: Clearly explaining the features and benefits of your product or service is essential for persuading potential customers of its worth. ChatGPT can help you develop concise and engaging descriptions that highlight the practical benefits of your offering while addressing the needs and desires of your target audience.
Prompt example: "List the top 5 features and benefits of an e-commerce training program in the 'make money' niche, focusing on how it can help users build and scale profitable online businesses."

5. Social Proof and Testimonials: Incorporating social proof and testimonials in your sales copy can bolster trust and credibility with your target audience while also demonstrating the effectiveness of your products or services. ChatGPT can assist you in creating compelling testimonials and case studies that exhibit the real-world impact of your offerings and persuade potential customers to invest.
Prompt example: "Write 3 testimonials for a dropshipping course in the 'make money' niche, emphasizing the positive results achieved by users who have completed the program."

6. Objections and Rebuttals: Addressing potential objections and concerns in your sales copy can enhance trust and credibility, increasing the likelihood that potential customers will act. ChatGPT can help you

identify common objections and craft thoughtful rebuttals that alleviate fears and provide reassurance.
Prompt example: "Identify 3 common objections to investing in an online course on passive income strategies and provide effective rebuttals for each objection."

7. A potent call to action (CTA) is essential for driving conversions and guiding potential customers toward the desired action. ChatGPT can help you create compelling CTAs that are clear, concise, and actionable, motivating your audience to move forward with your product or service.
Prompt example: "Write a persuasive call to action for a sales page promoting a membership site in the 'make money' niche, focusing on urgency, the benefits of joining, and the ease of signing up."

8. After your CTA, consider including post-CTA content that re-emphasizes the value of your offering, tackles any remaining objections, and supplies extra information or incentives to inspire potential customers to act. ChatGPT can aid you in crafting captivating post-CTA content that reinforces the advantages of your product or service and wins over wavering prospects.
Prompt example: "Create a post-call to action section for a sales page offering a cryptocurrency investment course in the 'make money' niche, including a summary of the key benefits, a limited-time bonus offer, and a reminder of the risk-free guarantee."

Businesses in the "make money" niche can produce convincing and persuasive content that connects with their target audience and boosts conversions by capitalizing on ChatGPT's capabilities in crafting sales copy. The AI's knack for generating targeted, engaging, and conversion-centric content makes it a valuable resource for crafting effective sales copy for any product or service.

Content creation examples and case studies

In this section, we'll explore some real-world examples and case studies of ChatGPT content creation. These instances showcase the AI's adaptability and efficacy in producing a diverse array of content types for businesses in the "make money" niche, ultimately supporting their growth and success.

1. ChatGPT was employed to generate high-quality, informative articles on subjects like budgeting, saving, and investing for a personal finance blog. By using ChatGPT to create well-researched and captivating content, the blog managed to draw in and retain a devoted audience, enhancing organic traffic and ad revenue over time.
Prompt example: "Write a comprehensive blog post on the benefits of dollar-cost averaging as a long-term investment strategy, including practical examples and tips for implementation."

2. An affiliate marketing expert utilized ChatGPT to develop engaging social media content to promote their products and services. By using AI to create attention-catching headlines, captions, and calls to action, they significantly boosted their social media engagement and directed more traffic to their website.
Prompt example: "Create a series of 5 social media post captions promoting an online course on building passive income streams, focusing on the key benefits and incorporating a sense of urgency."

3. A YouTuber in the "make money" niche harnessed ChatGPT to generate video scripts on an array of subjects such as online business models, marketing strategies, and growth hacking methods. They managed to create high-quality, appealing video content that resonated with their audience and helped grow their subscriber base by leveraging the AI's capabilities.
Prompt example: "Write a video script for a 10-minute tutorial on using Facebook ads to drive targeted traffic to an affiliate marketing website, including step-by-step instructions and practical tips for optimizing ad performance."

4. A digital marketing agency employed ChatGPT to create lead magnets and opt-in content for their clients in the "make money" niche. By developing high-value resources like eBooks, checklists, and templates, they assisted their clients in growing their email lists and nurturing leads more effectively.
Prompt example: "Create an outline for a comprehensive eBook on starting and scaling an e-commerce business, including key topics to cover, actionable tips, and case studies."

5. A business coach in the "make money" niche used ChatGPT to generate content for their online course on constructing profitable niche websites. The AI-generated course materials, encompassing video scripts, presentation slides, and worksheets, allowed them to offer their students a thorough and engaging learning experience.
Prompt example: "Design a detailed lesson plan for a module on keyword research and content planning for niche websites, including learning objectives, key concepts, and practical activities."

6. An online entrepreneur utilized ChatGPT to create a series of automated emails for their sales funnel, advertising their flagship product in the "make money" niche. By employing AI to generate persuasive and engaging email copy, they managed to boost their conversion rate and generate more sales.
Prompt example: "Write a 5-email sequence for a sales funnel promoting a high-ticket coaching program on building and scaling online businesses, focusing on the program's benefits, social proof, and addressing potential objections."

These real-world examples and case studies exemplify ChatGPT's capacity to generate content for businesses in the "make money" niche. By harnessing AI's ability to produce targeted, engaging, and convincing content across an extensive range of formats and platforms, businesses can streamline their content creation process, conserve time and resources, and ultimately drive growth and success.

Chapter 5. Mastering Content Marketing with ChatGPT

Planning content marketing strategies

Content marketing is a potent instrument for boosting brand awareness, attracting and retaining customers, and ultimately generating revenue in the fiercely competitive "make money" niche. A well-conceived strategy is necessary to optimize the efficacy of content marketing endeavors. ChatGPT can aid businesses in the "make money" niche with content marketing strategy planning and execution by conjuring up ideas, refining content for search engines, and crafting engaging content that resonates with their target audience. In this section, we'll discuss three content marketing strategies and provide some sample prompts for using ChatGPT to assist you.

1. Strategy 1: Buyer Persona-Specific Content. Grasping your target audience and producing content that caters to their particular needs and preferences is crucial for a triumphant content marketing campaign. By establishing buyer personas, you can create targeted content that directly addresses your audience, tackling their unique pain points, desires, and objectives.
Prompt example: "Generate a list of 10 blog post ideas for a personal finance website targeting millennials who are interested in passive income streams and financial independence. Focus on topics that address their specific needs, challenges, and aspirations."

2. Strategy 2: Content Pillars and Topic Clusters. Organizing your content marketing initiatives around content pillars and topic clusters can enhance your website's visibility and authority in search engine results. Topic clusters are related subtopics that link back to the pillar content, which are comprehensive pieces covering a core topic in depth. This tactic not only aids SEO but also delivers a consistent user experience for your target audience.
Prompt example: "Create an outline for a content pillar on affiliate marketing for a 'make money' niche website. Include the main sections,

key topics to cover, and a list of related topic clusters that can be linked back to the pillar content."

3. Strategy 3: Diversifying Content Formats. Diversifying your content formats enables you to engage a broader audience and cater to varying preferences and learning styles. By repurposing and adapting content across diverse formats like blog posts, videos, podcasts, infographics, and more, you can maximize the reach and impact of your content marketing efforts.
Prompt example: "Repurpose a blog post on dropshipping success stories into a compelling video script, focusing on the key takeaways, actionable tips, and engaging storytelling."

4. Strategy 4: Using Data-Driven Insights. Data-driven insights can help you spot trends, preferences, and opportunities to better engage your audience by informing your content marketing strategy. By examining metrics such as website traffic, social media engagement, and conversion rates, you can make informed decisions on content topics, formats, and distribution channels.
Prompt example: "Analyze the top-performing blog posts on a 'make money' niche website based on traffic and engagement data. Identify common themes, formats, and styles, and suggest 5 new content ideas based on these insights."

5. Strategy 5: Storytelling and Emotional Appeal. Incorporating storytelling and emotional appeal into your content can help you forge a deeper connection with your audience, making it more memorable and shareable. By crafting narratives that resonate with your target audience's experiences, values, and aspirations, you can enhance the effectiveness of your content marketing efforts.
Prompt example: "Write a compelling success story about a person who achieved financial freedom through investing in real estate. Focus on the challenges they faced, the strategies they employed, and the lessons learned along the way."

6. Strategy 6: Content Distribution and Promotion. A successful content marketing strategy encompasses not just the creation of top-notch content, but also its distribution and promotion. By leveraging various distribution channels such as email marketing, social media, and influencer partnerships, you can ensure your content reaches a larger audience and drives engagement.
Prompt example: "Develop a content distribution plan for a new blog post on building an online business, including a list of promotional channels, tactics, and a schedule for sharing the content across these channels."

7. Strategy 7: User-Generated Content and Social Proof. User-generated content (UGC) and social proof are effective methods for establishing trust and credibility with your target audience. By encouraging your audience to share their own experiences, success stories, and testimonials, you can create authentic and relatable content that resonates with potential customers.
Prompt example: "Create a campaign to encourage users of a 'make money' niche online course to share their success stories on social media, including a hashtag, contest, and incentives for participation."

8. Strategy 8: Consistent Branding and Messaging. Consistent branding and messaging across all your content help reinforce your brand identity and build trust with your audience. By ensuring your content is consistent with your brand's voice, style, and values, you can create a cohesive and memorable content marketing experience.
Prompt example: "Review and edit a series of blog posts for a 'make money' niche website to ensure consistent branding, messaging, and tone, focusing on key elements such as headlines, subheadings, and calls to action."

Businesses in the "make money" niche can create more effective and targeted content that resonates with their audience and drives results by leveraging

ChatGPT's capabilities in content marketing strategy planning. You can generate a wide range of content ideas with ChatGPT's help, organize content around content pillars and topic clusters, and diversify content formats for maximum reach and engagement.

SEO optimization

SEO (Search Engine Optimization) is a crucial aspect of any triumphant content marketing strategy, especially in the competitive "make money" niche. By optimizing your content for search engines, you can boost your website's visibility, increase organic traffic, and draw in more potential customers. ChatGPT can be an invaluable SEO partner, helping you craft keyword-rich content, fine-tune meta tags, and produce engaging, high-quality content that ranks well in search results. Here are some key aspects of ChatGPT SEO optimization:

1. Keyword Research and Integration: Identifying relevant and high-traffic keywords is vital for creating content that excels in search results. ChatGPT can aid you in developing a list of target keywords and weaving them naturally into your content, ensuring it's engaging for readers and search engine optimized.
Prompt example: "Generate a list of 10 relevant long-tail keywords for a blog post about creating passive income streams and provide suggestions for integrating these keywords into the content."

2. Optimizing Meta Tags: Meta tags, including title tags, meta descriptions, and header tags, play a crucial role in how search engines comprehend and rank your content. ChatGPT can help you create compelling, keyword-rich meta tags that entice users to click on your content in search results and boost your website's search ranking.
Prompt example: "Write an optimized title tag and meta description for a blog post about starting an e-commerce business using the keywords 'e-commerce business,' 'online store,' and 'entrepreneurship.'"

3. Crafting High-Quality, Engaging Content: Search engines reward content that provides value and relevance to users. By leveraging

ChatGPT, you can enhance your website's search ranking and drive more organic traffic by generating well-researched, comprehensive, and captivating content.

Prompt example: "Write a 1,500-word blog post about the top 10 online business models for generating passive income, focusing on providing valuable insights, actionable tips, and engaging storytelling."

4. Internal and External Linking: Strong internal and external linking structures are essential for SEO. ChatGPT can help you identify relevant internal links to incorporate within your content and recommend trustworthy external sources to reference, improving your website's overall quality and authority.

Prompt example: "Suggest 5 internal links to include in a blog post about affiliate marketing strategies, and provide a list of 3 reputable external sources to reference for additional information."

5. Optimizing Content for Featured Snippets: Featured snippets are highlighted search results displayed at the top of Google's search results page, offering a succinct answer to a user's query. By optimizing your content for featured snippets, you can boost your website's visibility and traffic. ChatGPT can assist in crafting well-structured, concise, and informative content that increases your chances of being featured in a snippet.

Prompt example: "Write a clear and concise answer to the question 'How do you start a successful dropshipping business?' that could be used as a featured snippet."

6. Image Optimization: Images play a significant role in user engagement and can also contribute to SEO. Image optimization enhances your website's search ranking and overall user experience by compressing images, using descriptive file names, and adding alt tags with pertinent keywords. ChatGPT can help you create keyword-rich, descriptive alt tags for your images.

Prompt example: "Generate alt tags for three images in a blog post about passive income: one image featuring a person working on a laptop, one image showing a chart of various income streams, and one image of a stack of books on finance."

7. Mobile-Friendliness and Page Speed: Ensuring your website is mobile-friendly and has swift-loading pages is vital for both user experience and SEO. Although ChatGPT can't directly help with technical aspects like website design and page speed optimization, it can aid in the creation of content that is easily readable and formatted for mobile devices.
Prompt example: "Review and edit a blog post on real estate investing for mobile-friendliness, focusing on formatting, readability, and breaking the content into easily digestible sections."

8. Content Refresh and Updating: Regularly updating and refreshing your existing content can help you maintain or improve your search ranking. ChatGPT can be used to identify out-of-date information, generate new insights, and update your content to keep it relevant and valuable for your audience.
Prompt example: "Review a blog post on cryptocurrency investing from 2021 and update it with the latest trends, developments, and best practices for investing in cryptocurrencies in 2023."

Businesses in the "make money" niche can create content that ranks higher in search results, attracts more organic traffic, and ultimately drives growth and success by harnessing ChatGPT's SEO optimization capabilities.

Social media and influencer marketing

Social media and influencer marketing have become crucial elements of successful content marketing strategies in today's digital world, particularly in the "make money" niche. Businesses can amplify the reach of their content, engage their target audience, and drive traffic and conversions by harnessing the power of social media platforms and partnering with influencers. ChatGPT can be an incredibly valuable tool for crafting engaging social media content, creating influencer outreach messages, and optimizing campaigns. Here are some ways ChatGPT can assist you with your social media and influencer marketing endeavors:

1. Creating Engaging Social Media Content: ChatGPT can help you produce eye-catching headlines, captions, and social media posts that resonate with your audience and encourage them to interact with your content.
Prompt example: "Write 5 engaging and creative Instagram captions for a series of posts promoting a 'make money' online course on affiliate marketing."

2. Hashtag Research and Strategy: Hashtags play a vital role in boosting the visibility of your content on social media platforms. ChatGPT can help you identify relevant and popular hashtags to use in your posts, ensuring that your content reaches a broader audience.
Prompt example: "Generate a list of 10 relevant hashtags for a Twitter post about passive income through stock market investing."

3. Crafting Influencer Outreach Messages: Collaborating with influencers can be an excellent way to raise brand awareness and expose your content to a larger audience. ChatGPT can help you create personalized and persuasive outreach messages that capture the attention of influencers and boost the chances of fruitful collaborations.
Prompt example: "Write a personalized email to a finance influencer, inviting them to collaborate on a YouTube video about building a successful e-commerce business."

4. Developing Influencer Marketing Campaign Ideas: ChatGPT can be an excellent source of inspiration for devising unique and engaging influencer marketing campaign ideas that appeal to both the influencer's audience and your target demographic.

Prompt example: "Generate 3 creative influencer marketing campaign ideas for promoting a new 'make money' online course focused on real estate investing."

5. Monitoring and Analyzing Campaign Performance: While ChatGPT cannot directly help you monitor and analyze the performance of your social media and influencer marketing campaigns, it can assist you in creating reports, summaries, and insights based on the data you provide.
Prompt example: "Write a summary of the performance of a recent influencer marketing campaign for a 'make money' coaching program, including key metrics such as reach, engagement, and conversions."

6. Optimizing Social Media Profiles: A well-optimized social media profile can enhance your brand's online presence and make it easier for your target audience to discover and connect with you. ChatGPT can help you craft compelling profile descriptions and bios that incorporate relevant keywords and effectively convey your brand message.
Prompt example: "Write an optimized LinkedIn company page description for a digital marketing agency specializing in the 'make money' niche."

7. Planning and Scheduling Content: Consistency in posting and engagement are vital components of a successful social media presence. ChatGPT can help you create a content calendar or schedule for your social media posts, ensuring that you consistently share top-notch content at the best times for your audience.
Prompt example: "Create a 4-week social media content plan for promoting a 'make money' podcast on Facebook, Twitter, and Instagram, including post ideas, captions, and posting frequency."

8. Engaging with Your Audience: Long-term success in social media marketing hinges on a strong relationship with your followers and influencers. ChatGPT can help you generate personalized and engaging

responses to your audience's comments and messages, fostering a sense of community and loyalty.

Prompt example: "Provide 5 engaging responses to comments from followers on a recent Instagram post about a blog article discussing passive income strategies."

Businesses in the "make money" niche can create more captivating and effective campaigns by incorporating ChatGPT's capabilities into their social media and influencer marketing efforts, ultimately leading to increased brand awareness, traffic, and conversions. By utilizing ChatGPT's assistance in crafting compelling content, building meaningful relationships with influencers, and engaging with their target audience, businesses can set themselves apart in the competitive online space and achieve long-term success.

Successful content marketing examples

In this section, we will explore examples of thriving content marketing in the "make money" niche. These instances illustrate how various content marketing approaches and techniques can be employed to boost traffic, engage audiences, and spark conversions.

1. ChatGPT-Generated Finance Blog: A personal finance blog in the "make money" niche successfully utilized ChatGPT to create a series of high-quality, informative articles on topics like investing, saving money, and debt management. The blog owner employed ChatGPT to create outlines, draft articles, and even devise attention-grabbing headlines. By leveraging ChatGPT's capabilities, the blog owner consistently produced engaging content, resulting in increased traffic and conversions.
Prompt example: "Generate an outline for a blog post on 5 effective ways to save money for a down payment on a house."

2. Online Course Promotion with ChatGPT: An entrepreneur offering an online course on affiliate marketing used ChatGPT to create a comprehensive content marketing strategy. This included crafting persuasive email campaigns, engaging social media posts, and compelling

ad copy. Consequently, course enrollment and overall revenue saw significant growth. The entrepreneur credited ChatGPT's ability to generate high-quality, persuasive content that resonated with their target audience as a key factor in their success.

Prompt example: "Write a persuasive email campaign introducing a new online course on affiliate marketing and highlighting its benefits."

3. ChatGPT-Powered Influencer Collaboration: A "make money" niche expert collaborated with ChatGPT to create a series of guest blog posts for high-traffic websites. They used ChatGPT to create outlines, drafts, and finalized articles tailored to each website's style and audience. This led to greater exposure, increased website traffic, and new business opportunities. The expert attributed their success to ChatGPT's ability to adapt to different writing styles and create content that was relevant to the audience and tone of each website.

Prompt example: "Create a guest blog post on the importance of financial planning for millennials, tailored to the audience of a popular personal finance website."

4. Social Media Content Generation with ChatGPT: A financial coaching company employed ChatGPT to create engaging social media content aimed at helping their followers make better financial decisions. After using ChatGPT to generate informative and relatable social media posts, captions, and responses to comments, the company saw a significant increase in followers and engagement rates. ChatGPT's success was attributed to its ability to create content that resonated with their audience while also fostering a sense of community.

Prompt example: "Generate 10 engaging social media post ideas for a financial coaching business focused on helping individuals make better financial decisions."

5. ChatGPT-Enhanced Video Scripts for YouTube: A YouTuber in the "make money" niche used ChatGPT to create engaging and informative

video scripts for their channel. They suggested topics to ChatGPT, and the AI generated detailed scripts that captured key points while maintaining a conversational and engaging tone. This resulted in higher viewer retention, a growing subscriber base, and increased ad revenue for the YouTuber.

Prompt example: "Write a script for a 10-minute YouTube video explaining the basics of stock market investing for beginners."

6. E-book Writing and Editing with ChatGPT: An author employed ChatGPT to create an e-book about generating passive income through real estate investments. They used ChatGPT to create the first drafts of each chapter, which they then edited and refined for consistency and accuracy. This method significantly reduced the time and effort required to create the e-book, resulting in a shorter time to market and higher sales.

Prompt example: "Create an outline for an e-book on generating passive income through real estate investments, including chapter titles and key points."

These examples demonstrate how businesses in the "make money" niche can reap substantial benefits by incorporating ChatGPT into their content marketing efforts. You can use ChatGPT to create high-quality, engaging, and actionable content that will help you build brand authority, connect with your audience, and drive results. By leveraging the power of ChatGPT, you can stay ahead of the competition and create a lasting impact in your niche, ultimately leading to increased brand awareness, customer loyalty, and conversions.

Chapter 6. Monitoring Performance and Analytics

Setting up KPIs

Monitoring performance is vital in the realm of content marketing and online business to comprehend the effectiveness of your tactics and make data-driven decisions. KPIs are quantifiable values that aid businesses in tracking their advancement toward specific objectives. By establishing relevant KPIs, you can evaluate whether your efforts are producing the desired outcomes and pinpoint areas for enhancement.

Selecting the Optimal KPIs:
Picking the right KPIs for your content marketing endeavors and business strategies is crucial for accurately gauging the success of your campaigns and tactics. The KPIs you opt for should be closely connected to your overarching business goals and offer insight into the efficacy of your marketing efforts. Here are some prevalent KPIs in the "make money" niche:

1. Website traffic: Monitoring the number of people who visit your website can help you assess the reach and effectiveness of your content marketing initiatives.
   Prompt example: "Suggest a list of important KPIs for a content marketing campaign in the 'make money' niche."

2. Conversion rate: This KPI measures the percentage of website visitors who complete a desired action, such as signing up for a newsletter, purchasing a product, or joining an online course.
   Prompt example: "Provide industry benchmarks for email marketing campaigns in the 'make money' niche, including open rates, click-through rates, and conversion rates."

3. Engagement metrics: Metrics like time on site, bounce rate, and pages per session can offer insights into how well your content resonates with your audience.

Prompt example: "What are the best practices for setting up and monitoring KPIs for a social media marketing campaign in the 'make money' niche?"

4. Social media metrics: Keeping track of the growth and engagement of your social media channels, such as followers, likes, shares, and comments, can help you evaluate the success of your social media marketing endeavors.
Prompt example: "Explain how to create a custom dashboard in Google Analytics to monitor KPIs related to website traffic and user engagement in the 'make money' niche."

5. Email marketing metrics: KPIs like open rates, click-through rates, and conversion rates are crucial for gauging the efficacy of your email marketing campaigns.
Prompt example: "Describe the process of setting targets for KPIs in a content marketing campaign and how to adjust these targets over time based on performance data."

6. Return on investment (ROI): Computing the ROI of your marketing efforts is essential for determining campaign profitability and ensuring efficient resource allocation.
Prompt example: "Provide a step-by-step guide on analyzing email marketing campaign performance and identifying areas for improvement using key metrics in the 'make money' niche."

Establishing Goals and Benchmarks:
After you've determined which KPIs are ideal for your business, you must set benchmarks and goals for each metric. Benchmarks are industry norms or your own company's historical data that can be employed to assess your performance. Setting targets involves determining the desired level of performance for each KPI and establishing a timeframe for accomplishing those objectives.

KPIs for Monitoring and Reporting:

Regularly monitoring your KPIs is crucial for staying informed about your marketing efforts' performance and making data-driven choices. You can use various tools and platforms, such as Google Analytics, social media analytics, and email marketing platforms, to track your KPIs. Creating custom dashboards and reports can also help you visualize performance data and effortlessly share insights with your team.

By setting KPIs, establishing benchmarks, and monitoring your performance data, you can effectively measure your content marketing campaigns' success and make informed decisions to refine your strategies in the "make money" niche.

Leveraging ChatGPT for data analysis

Businesses need to sift through and interpret vast amounts of data to gain insights and fine-tune their strategies in the era of data-driven decision-making. With its sophisticated natural language processing capabilities, ChatGPT can be an invaluable tool for scrutinizing data and generating actionable insights, particularly in the "make money" niche. By utilizing ChatGPT for data analysis, you can save time, enhance accuracy, and gain a deeper understanding of your marketing performance.

Examining Performance Data with ChatGPT:
ChatGPT can delve into a variety of performance data, encompassing website traffic, social media engagement, and email marketing metrics. By supplying ChatGPT with your raw data or a summary of your performance data, you can obtain thorough and extensive analyses that spotlight trends, patterns, and areas for enhancement.

For instance, you can direct ChatGPT to analyze your website traffic data and pinpoint the most effective traffic sources or content. Likewise, you can employ ChatGPT to evaluate your social media performance and identify the types of posts that most resonate with your target audience.

You can use the following prompts to kick off with ChatGPT for data analysis:

1. "Analyze the website traffic data for the past three months and identify the top three sources of traffic and their respective conversion rates."
2. "Evaluate the performance of our email marketing campaign for the past month, including open rates, click-through rates, and conversions, and suggest areas for improvement."
3. "Based on our social media engagement data for the past quarter, which types of content generate the most likes, shares, and comments?"

Generating Insights and Offering Recommendations:
In addition to analyzing performance data, ChatGPT can provide insights and recommendations for enhancing your marketing strategies. By posing specific questions about your KPIs or areas of concern to ChatGPT, you can obtain actionable suggestions for optimizing your campaigns.

For example, you can use ChatGPT to generate ideas for improving your website's conversion rate, boosting email open rates, or augmenting engagement on your social media channels.

Here are some ideas to help you get started:

1. "What are some effective strategies for increasing website conversion rates in the 'make money' niche?"
2. "Provide suggestions for improving email open rates and click-through rates for our 'make money' newsletter."
3. "What types of content can help drive more engagement and growth on our social media channels in the 'make money' niche?"

By harnessing ChatGPT for data analysis and insight generation, you can improve your decision-making process, fine-tune your marketing strategies, and ultimately achieve superior results in the "make money" niche.

Adapting and refining strategies

To stay competitive and reach their goals in the ever-evolving landscape of the "make money" niche, businesses must continuously adapt and fine-tune their marketing strategies. By leveraging ChatGPT for data analysis and insights, you can pinpoint areas for improvement, generate fresh ideas, and optimize your campaigns without the need for API integration. This section will guide you through the process of transferring data to ChatGPT and harnessing its capabilities to adapt and refine your strategies.

Sharing Data with ChatGPT:
To share data with ChatGPT and gain valuable insights, simply input your data, summaries, or questions as text prompts. ChatGPT's text-based chat interface enables you to offer context, pose questions, and request analyses of your marketing performance data. This approach doesn't necessitate any API integration and can be employed directly via ChatGPT-enabled chat platforms or web interfaces.

Here are some examples of data sharing with ChatGPT:

1. Rather than supplying raw data, you can present summarized information about your marketing performance. For instance, you could input a concise summary of your website traffic, conversion rates, or social media engagement metrics.

2. Pose specific questions: You can query ChatGPT about your marketing performance or areas of concern. This method yields targeted insights and recommendations without needing you to share copious amounts of data.

Adapting Strategies in Response to Insights:
Upon sharing your data with ChatGPT and acquiring insights into your marketing performance, you can start adjusting your strategies accordingly. This process involves the following steps:

1. Identifying areas for improvement: Utilize ChatGPT insights to detect aspects of your marketing campaigns that warrant optimization. This might encompass underperforming content, lackluster traffic sources, or ineffective marketing channels.

2. Generating new ideas: Engage ChatGPT to produce new marketing concepts and tactics addressing the identified areas for improvement. This could involve experimenting with novel content formats, targeting different audience segments, or using alternative marketing channels.

3. Implementing changes: Apply ChatGPT's insights and recommendations to make necessary alterations to your marketing campaigns. This might entail revising your content strategy, fine-tuning your targeting, or adjusting your marketing budget allocation.

4. Monitoring results: Continuously track the performance of your adapted strategies using your KPIs and other relevant metrics. This enables you to evaluate the effectiveness of your changes and pinpoint any further improvements that may be needed.

5. Iterating the process: Adapting and refining strategies is an ongoing endeavor. Keep consulting ChatGPT for insights and make any required adjustments to your marketing campaigns as you gather new performance data.

Here are some examples of ChatGPT prompts to assist you in adapting and refining your strategies:

1. "Based on the insights provided earlier about our website traffic, what alterations can we make to our content strategy to draw more visitors from our top-performing traffic sources?"

2. "Taking into account our email marketing campaign performance, how can we enhance our email subject lines and content to boost open rates and click-through rates?"

3. "With our social media engagement data in mind, what types of posts can we craft to elicit more likes, shares, and comments from our target audience in the 'make money' niche?"

By employing ChatGPT to analyze your marketing performance data and generate actionable insights, you can effectively adapt and refine your strategies to achieve superior results in the "make money" niche. This iterative process will aid you in staying ahead of the competition.

Performance monitoring examples

In this section, we'll demonstrate how businesses can harness ChatGPT to monitor marketing performance and tweak their strategies accordingly.

1. Example 1: Performance Analysis of a Blog Post
   A business owner in the "make money" niche wants to evaluate the performance of their blog posts over the past six months. They supply a summary of their blog's traffic data to ChatGPT, including the top-performing posts, traffic sources, and average time spent on each post.
   Prompt: "Analyze our blog's performance over the last six months, and provide insights on which topics and post types performed best and why."
   ChatGPT generates an in-depth analysis based on the given data, pinpointing the most successful topics and post types, as well as potential reasons behind their success. The business owner can then utilize these insights to fine-tune their content strategy and concentrate on producing more of the high-performing content types.

2. Example 2: Social Media Campaign Adjustment
   A digital marketer is managing a social media campaign for a client in the "make money" niche. They observe that the engagement on their recent

posts promoting a new product is lower than in previous campaigns. The marketer shares the engagement data with ChatGPT and requests insights and suggestions.

Prompt: "Our recent social media posts promoting a new product have garnered lower engagement than previous campaigns. What could be the reasons for this, and how can we enhance our social media strategy to boost engagement?"

ChatGPT identifies several possible reasons for the diminished engagement, including post format, timing, and messaging. The digital marketer then implements ChatGPT's recommendations, adjusting post format, timing, and messaging to better connect with their target audience. They persistently monitor engagement data and make modifications as needed, ultimately achieving improved performance for their social media campaign.

3. Example 3: Email Marketing Optimization

   An online course creator in the "make money" niche wants to improve their email marketing performance.

   Prompt: "Our email open rates and click-through rates are lower than we'd like. Can you provide suggestions for enhancing these metrics in our 'make money' online course promotion emails?"

   ChatGPT offers several recommendations, such as refining subject lines, personalizing email content, and segmenting the audience for more targeted messaging. The course creator implements these changes and closely tracks the results, observing a significant increase in both open and click-through rates for their promotional emails.

These examples illustrate how companies in the "make money" niche can employ ChatGPT to keep tabs on marketing performance.

Chapter 7. Scaling Your Business with ChatGPT

Identifying New Markets

Scaling your business in the "make money" niche requires uncovering new markets and opportunities for growth. ChatGPT can be a helpful ally in this pursuit, as it can aid you in analyzing historical market trends, pinpointing potential target segments, and exploring emerging opportunities up until its knowledge cutoff date in September 2021. In this section, we'll discuss how to utilize ChatGPT to discover new markets and expand your reach, while also recognizing its limitations and anticipating future updates that could deliver real-time trend data.

Recognizing Market Trends:
Staying on top of market trends is crucial for identifying new opportunities in the "make money" niche. Although ChatGPT's knowledge is restricted to September 2021, it can still offer insights into historical trends, burgeoning industries, and popular business models up to that point. You can use this information as a launchpad for further research, allowing you to search for continuations or evolutions of these trends in the present.

Here are some examples of prompts to help you understand market trends using ChatGPT:

1. "What were the most popular trends in the 'make money' niche up to 2021?"
2. "Which industries experienced rapid growth up to 2021 and might still be relevant for businesses in the 'make money' niche?"
3. "What types of business models were gaining popularity in the 'make money' niche up to 2021?"

ChatGPT will become an even more potent tool for businesses seeking to identify new markets and opportunities once it is updated to provide real-time trend information.

Identifying Target Audiences:

Expanding your business often involves reaching new target segments. ChatGPT can help you in identifying prospective customer segments who may be interested in your products or services. By asking ChatGPT about different demographics, interests, or pain points up to its knowledge cutoff date, you can discover new customer groups to target.

Here are some prompts for identifying target segments with ChatGPT:

1. "What demographic groups were most likely to be interested in 'make money' products or services up to 2021?"
2. "What types of interests or hobbies might be associated with potential customers in the 'make money' niche up to 2021?"
3. "What were the common pain points or challenges faced by individuals in the 'make money' niche up to 2021?"

Investigating Emerging Opportunities:

ChatGPT can also support you in exploring new opportunities in the "make money" niche by providing ideas for innovative products, services, or marketing strategies up to its knowledge cutoff date. You can uncover new avenues for growth by asking ChatGPT about potential market gaps or fresh approaches to addressing customer needs.

Use the following prompts to investigate new opportunities with ChatGPT:

1. "What were some potential gaps in the market within the 'make money' niche up to 2021 that we can capitalize on?"
2. "What innovative products or services could be developed to address customer needs in the 'make money' niche up to 2021?"
3. "How can we differentiate our business from competitors in the 'make money' niche and capture a larger market share up to 2021?"

By leveraging ChatGPT's insights and analysis on historical trends and combining them with your own research on current market developments, you can identify new markets, target segments, and emerging opportunities in the "make money" niche. This will enable you to broaden your reach, increase your customer base, and ultimately achieve success in scaling your business.

Expanding product/service offerings

As your business grows, it's crucial to expand your product or service offerings to address the shifting needs of your customers and stay competitive in the "make money" niche. ChatGPT can help you generate new ideas, fine-tune existing offerings, and pinpoint areas for improvement. However, bear in mind that ChatGPT's knowledge is limited to data up to September 2021. In this section, we'll explore how to use ChatGPT to broaden your product or service offerings while considering data limitations, so you can continue meeting the demands of your target market.

New Idea Generation:
ChatGPT is a fantastic resource for brainstorming new product or service ideas. By asking open-ended questions or providing specific criteria, you can obtain a wide array of suggestions for your next offering. This can aid you in diversifying your portfolio and catering to a broader audience. Keep in mind that ChatGPT's recommendations will be based on data up to 2021, so you'll need to verify and update any information as necessary.

Here are some ideas for new products or services to help you brainstorm with ChatGPT:

1. "What are some innovative product ideas for the 'make money' niche that were popular up to 2021 and may still be relevant today?"
2. "What types of services were in high demand in the 'make money' niche up to 2021 and could complement our existing offerings?"
3. "What were some unique and creative ways to package our current products or services to appeal to a new target market up to 2021?"

Refining Current Offerings:

Constantly enhancing and refining your existing products or services is crucial to keeping them relevant and enticing to your customers. ChatGPT can help you identify areas for improvement and recommend ways to enhance your offerings based on customer feedback or market trends up until 2021. Don't forget to validate and update the ChatGPT information, as it might not reflect the latest market shifts.

Use the following prompts to help you fine-tune your existing ChatGPT product or service offerings:

1. "Based on customer feedback up to 2021, what were some common issues with our current product/service that we can improve?"
2. "What features or benefits could we add to our existing product/service to make it more competitive in the 'make money' niche, considering trends up to 2021?"
3. "How can we update our current product/service to better align with emerging trends in the 'make money' niche that were observed up to 2021?"

Identifying Related Products/Services:
Introducing complementary products or services to your existing lineup is another way to expand your product or service offerings. Drawing on data through 2021, ChatGPT can help you identify opportunities for cross-selling, upselling, or creating bundled offerings that deliver added value to your customers.

Here are some ideas to help you find complementary products or services to use with ChatGPT:

1. "What complementary products/services were popular in the 'make money' niche up to 2021 that we could consider offering to our existing customers?"

2. "What types of bundled offerings were successful up to 2021 and could provide more value to our customers and increase our average transaction value?"
3. "How can we leverage our existing products/services to cross-sell or upsell additional offerings to our customers based on trends up to 2021?"

By using ChatGPT to brainstorm new ideas, refine your current offerings, and identify complementary products or services, you can expand your product or service lineup and meet the evolving needs of your customers.

Building a sustainable business model

Building a long-term business model is essential for enduring success in the "make money" niche. A well-thought-out business model guarantees that your company stays profitable, adapts to market shifts, and continues to satisfy its customers. Despite a data limit of 2021, ChatGPT can be a useful asset in this process, helping you analyze various aspects of your business and providing insights for enhancement. In this section, we'll examine how to use ChatGPT to establish a sustainable business model while taking data constraints into account.

Revenue Stream Analysis:
Identifying and optimizing your revenue streams is a vital component of a sustainable business model. ChatGPT can help you evaluate your present revenue sources based on historical data and trends, as well as suggesting new ones that may have emerged before 2021. By diversifying your revenue streams, you can mitigate risks and ensure a steady flow of income.

Here are some questions to ponder when analyzing and optimizing revenue streams with ChatGPT:

1. "What were the most common revenue streams in the 'make money' niche before 2021, and how can we improve them to increase profitability?"
2. "What potential new revenue streams could we explore in the 'make money' niche based on pre-2021 trends?"

3. "How can we diversify our revenue streams to reduce dependency on a single source of income?"

Cost and Expense Optimization:

Efficient cost and expense management is crucial for maintaining a sustainable business model. Based on best practices and trends through 2021, ChatGPT can help you identify areas where you can trim costs or improve efficiency without compromising quality or customer satisfaction. This will assist you in increasing your profit margins and ensuring your company's long-term viability.

Use the following prompts to help you optimize your costs and expenses when using ChatGPT:

1. "What were the best practices for optimizing expenses in the 'make money' niche before 2021, and how can we apply them to reduce costs without impacting quality?"
2. "What cost-saving measures were successful in our business operations up to 2021, and how can we improve them to be more efficient?"
3. "How can we streamline our processes based on pre-2021 trends to reduce operational expenses while maintaining customer satisfaction?"

Increasing Customer Loyalty:

Customer loyalty is key to the long-term viability of your business. Repeat business, referrals, and valuable feedback from loyal customers can help you refine your products or services. ChatGPT can aid you in developing customer loyalty strategies based on historical data and best practices, such as broadening your offerings, improving customer service, or creating loyalty programs.

Here are some suggestions for increasing customer loyalty with ChatGPT:

1. "What strategies were effective for improving customer retention and loyalty in the 'make money' niche before 2021?"

2. "How can we enhance our customer support based on best practices up to 2021 to increase customer satisfaction and loyalty?"
3. "What types of loyalty programs or incentives were popular and successful before 2021 that we can implement to encourage repeat business and referrals?"

Adapting to Market Conditions:
The "make money" niche is constantly evolving, and a viable business model must be flexible to these changes. ChatGPT can keep you informed on market trends up to 2021, as well as offer insights on how to adjust your business model based on historical data. By staying adaptable, you can keep your business competitive and relevant in the long run.

With ChatGPT, use the following prompts to help you adjust your business model to market shifts:

1. "What were the current trends in the 'make money' niche before 2021, and how can we adapt our business model to capitalize on them?"
2. "How can we continuously monitor and adjust our product/service offerings to stay relevant in the 'make money' niche?"
3. "What strategies can we implement to ensure our business model remains agile and adaptable to market changes?"

By using ChatGPT to analyze revenue streams, optimize costs, build customer loyalty, and adapt to market changes, you can develop a sustainable business model that ensures long-term success in the "make money" niche.

Examples of successful scaling

In this section, we'll explore real-world examples of businesses that have successfully scaled their operations by leveraging ChatGPT-like tools. These case studies highlight how AI-powered assistance has helped businesses identify new markets, expand their offerings, and create sustainable business models.

1. Example 1: An e-learning platform. An online course platform specializing in the "make money" niche used ChatGPT to uncover new markets and broaden its course selection. They tapped into ChatGPT to investigate emerging trends, discovering a growing interest in cryptocurrency and blockchain technology courses. The platform then asked ChatGPT for advice on crafting a comprehensive curriculum and marketing strategy to attract students. As a result, the platform experienced a significant boost in user base and revenue.

   Prompt example: "What are the key topics we should include in a cryptocurrency and blockchain course, and how can we market it effectively to attract students?"

2. Example 2: Affiliate Marketing Company. Eager to diversify its product offerings and engage new customers, an affiliate marketing company turned to ChatGPT to identify fresh niches and high-growth products. After pinpointing a high-demand niche, they asked ChatGPT to help them devise a content strategy for their website, focusing on SEO-optimized articles, captivating social media content, and targeted email campaigns. This approach led to a considerable uptick in the company's traffic, conversions, and overall revenue.

   Prompt example: "What are some high-demand niches for affiliate marketing, and how can we develop a content strategy to promote products in this niche effectively?"

3. Example 3: Dropshipping Store. Aiming to expand its business, a dropshipping company sought new markets and high-growth products by using ChatGPT to delve into emerging consumer behaviors and preferences. They uncovered a rising interest in environmentally friendly and sustainable products, prompting them to ask ChatGPT for assistance in identifying trendy eco-friendly items and developing marketing strategies aimed at environmentally conscious consumers. As a result, the store successfully broadened its product offerings, attracted a new customer base, and enjoyed increased sales and revenue.

Prompt example: "What are some popular eco-friendly products we can add to our dropshipping store, and how can we market them to environmentally conscious consumers?"

These examples showcase the power of ChatGPT in scaling businesses within the "make money" niche. By harnessing AI-powered tools like ChatGPT, companies can pinpoint new opportunities, extend their offerings, and establish long-term business models.

Chapter 8. ChatGPT-4

Key differences between ChatGPT-4 and GPT-3

OpenAI's ChatGPT-4 and GPT-3 language models are both impressive, but there are key distinctions between them that make each better suited for different applications in the "make money" niche.

1. Refined language understanding: ChatGPT-4 has been designed with a more nuanced grasp of human language, allowing it to produce more accurate and coherent responses. This enhanced language comprehension is particularly helpful when crafting content or brainstorming ideas for businesses in the "make money" niche, as it leads to higher-quality output.

2. Superior context handling: ChatGPT-4 outperforms GPT-3 in context handling capabilities, enabling it to maintain context throughout a conversation or piece of content. This attribute is crucial for businesses aiming to create consistent and logical content, as it ensures the generated text remains cohesive and pertinent.

3. Expansive knowledge base: While both models have a knowledge cutoff date of 2021, ChatGPT-4 has been trained on a larger dataset, affording it a more comprehensive knowledge base. This increased knowledge can be especially advantageous for businesses in the "make money" niche, as it allows ChatGPT-4 to generate more informed and diverse insights.

4. Greater adaptability: ChatGPT-4 is designed to be more adaptable to a range of tasks and industries. Its flexibility makes it an outstanding choice for businesses in the "make money" niche, as it can be more readily customized to tackle specific challenges and generate content tailored to the industry's unique requirements.

When to Choose ChatGPT-4 over GPT-3

Deciding between ChatGPT-4 and GPT-3 in the "make money" niche boils down to the complexity of your tasks, the caliber of content required, and the level of analysis needed. ChatGPT-4, with its enhanced language comprehension, context retention, and response generation capabilities, is a better fit for businesses and users in this competitive niche who demand more precise and in-depth insights.

For instance, ChatGPT-4's advanced capabilities will be more advantageous if you're crafting content on complex financial subjects, devising intricate marketing plans, or seeking thorough competitor evaluations. Additionally, due to its superior ability to grasp and process complicated information, ChatGPT-4 is the go-to choice for more sophisticated brainstorming sessions for business ideas or support in creating comprehensive business strategies and growth plans.

GPT-3, conversely, might still be suitable for simpler tasks within the "make money" niche, such as producing basic content, managing elementary customer inquiries, or offering general financial guidance. If your requirements are less demanding and your resources are limited, GPT-3 could suffice.

In conclusion, ChatGPT-4 is the optimal choice for the "make money" niche when higher-quality content, more accurate data, and superior handling of complex tasks are needed. GPT-3, on the other hand, may be a practical option if your needs are more basic and your resources are constrained. Always take into account your specific needs and desired results before making a decision.

Appendix A – The Act Mode of ChatGPT

Requesting ChatGPT to "act" as a specific professional before responding can be advantageous for several reasons:

1. Context: Providing a particular professional context helps the AI model better comprehend the perspective you're seeking in the response. This ensures the information you get is relevant and applicable to the profession or field you're interested in.

2. Expertise: Different professionals possess varying areas of expertise, and specifying a professional role can result in more accurate and detailed information tailored to that profession's knowledge base. This assists you in receiving more precise answers to your inquiries.

3. Terminology and Jargon: Each profession has its own jargon and terminology. Instructing ChatGPT to act as a specific professional allows you to receive responses that use the proper language and terminology, making the information easier to understand and apply within that field's context.

4. Problem-solving approach: Professionals tackle problems and situations from different angles. By specifying a professional role, you gain insight into how someone in that profession might address a specific issue or question.

5. Limitations and Bias: AI models like ChatGPT may have comprehension limitations or provide biased information. Specifying a professional role increases the likelihood of receiving information consistent with that profession's standards and practices, helping to mitigate potential biases and inaccuracies.

You can ask ChatGPT to examine statements, books, or other content and provide a review from the perspective of a specific professional using the "act" mode. This helps you gain insights from a particular point of view or understand how someone with that expertise might interpret or analyze the content.

However, there are a few points to consider:

1. While ChatGPT can offer a general overview or analysis of the content, it may not capture all nuances or provide an in-depth review as a true professional with years of experience would. Also, it might not always supply accurate or up-to-date information, so it's crucial to independently verify the details.

2. Subjectivity: Since reviews and opinions are subjective, the AI's response might not represent every professional's perspective in that field. Understand that the analysis provided by ChatGPT is based on patterns in the text data it's been trained on and may not signify a universally accepted viewpoint.

3. Limited content access: If you request a review or analysis of a book or content published after ChatGPT's knowledge cutoff date (September 2021), the AI may not have access to the specifics of that work. In such cases, the AI may generate a response based on similar works or general field knowledge, which might not be entirely accurate or relevant.

In conclusion, using the "act" mode can be helpful for obtaining an initial analysis or perspective from a specific professional viewpoint. Keep in mind that ChatGPT is an AI model, not a real professional. Its responses are based on patterns in the training text data, and it may not always provide accurate or up-to-date information. Always double-check the information you receive from others.

Appendix B – ChatGPT Supported Writing Styles

The remarkable versatility of ChatGPT, a cutting-edge AI language model, allows it to support a plethora of writing styles, catering to a wide array of user needs and preferences. The ability to adapt its writing style makes ChatGPT an invaluable tool for generating content, gathering information, and exploring creative writing across numerous styles and tones. Some of the writing styles that ChatGPT can accommodate include narrative, descriptive, expository, persuasive, academic, technical, formal, informal, and creative writing. Additionally, it can adjust its tone to be professional, friendly, or humorous, as per the user's request.

To elicit a specific writing style or tone from ChatGPT, users should clearly indicate their preference within the prompt. This can be achieved by explicitly mentioning the desired style, tone, or any other relevant characteristic in the response. For instance, if a user wants ChatGPT to provide a descriptive response, they could ask, "Please explain the process of photosynthesis in a detailed and vivid manner." If a user is interested in a persuasive tone, they could request, "Argue in favor of adopting a plant-based diet, emphasizing its benefits and addressing common concerns."

For users who prefer informal writing or a casual tone, simply using a casual tone or informal language in the question can be effective, such as, "Hey, can you tell me why people are so into superhero movies?" The AI will adjust its response accordingly, generating content that aligns with the user's expectations.

ChatGPT's adaptability also extends to specific formats like poems, short stories, or articles. To receive a response in the preferred format, users should specify it in their prompt. For example, "Write a short poem about the beauty of autumn," or "Compose a news article discussing the impact of artificial intelligence on the job market." Providing clear instructions in the prompt ensures that the AI understands the user's expectations and generates a response that meets their requirements.

Furthermore, users can make their prompts more effective by incorporating examples, setting a word limit, or asking for a specific structure. For instance, if a user wants ChatGPT to write a formal letter, they could say, "Write a formal letter to the mayor expressing concerns about the lack of green spaces in the city, following a standard letter format." This level of detail allows ChatGPT to generate a response that closely aligns with the user's desired outcome.

While ChatGPT's versatility is impressive, it is important to remember that it may not always be perfect or capture every nuance in the way a human writer would. Nevertheless, its adaptability makes it a valuable tool for a wide range of writing tasks and purposes.

In summary, ChatGPT can support a multitude of writing styles and tones, making it a valuable resource for users with diverse requirements. To activate a specific writing style or tone, users must provide clear and concise instructions within their prompt, specifying the desired style, tone, format, or any other characteristic relevant to their request. This guidance will help ChatGPT generate responses that meet user expectations and cater to their unique needs.

By harnessing the power of AI and combining it with human creativity, ChatGPT can help users unlock new opportunities in various domains, such as content creation, idea generation, and problem-solving. Whether it is generating compelling marketing materials, engaging social media content, or thought-provoking blog posts, ChatGPT's ability to adapt to different writing styles and tones allows it to assist users across a broad spectrum of tasks and projects. As AI continues to advance and become more sophisticated, ChatGPT's capabilities in supporting various writing styles are likely to expand further, offering even more potential for users to explore and benefit from.

Appendix C – Bonus 200 Exclusive ChatGPT Prompts

As a special thank you for purchasing this book, we're delighted to offer you access to 200 exclusive ChatGPT prompts that can help you unlock the full potential of ChatGPT for your business. To claim your bonus, simply scan the QR code included in this book. With these carefully crafted prompts at your disposal, you'll have a valuable toolset that can guide you in generating innovative ideas, optimizing marketing strategies, creating high-quality content, and scaling your business to new heights. Don't miss out on this incredible opportunity to supercharge your journey to success in the "make money" niche!

Conclusion

In this book, we delved into ChatGPT's potential as a potent tool for businesses operating in the "make money" niche. We've explored how ChatGPT can be employed to create content, brainstorm ideas, devise marketing strategies, analyze competitors, track performance, and scale operations. Despite ChatGPT's data only extending up to 2021, it remains exceedingly valuable for providing insightful information and guidance to businesses seeking growth and success in their respective niches.

Throughout the book, we've touched upon various techniques and tactics for harnessing ChatGPT's capabilities to enhance and automate business processes. We've offered numerous real-world examples and case studies illustrating ChatGPT's potential impact across different business sectors. Additionally, we've shared several prompts to help users effectively engage with ChatGPT and extract valuable insights.

It's crucial to recognize that ChatGPT isn't a magical solution that will instantly resolve all business challenges. However, when used properly and strategically, it's a powerful tool that can significantly boost a business's efficiency and efficacy. Companies in the "make money" niche can capitalize on the immense potential of technology by embracing AI-powered assistants like ChatGPT.

As ChatGPT and other AI tools progress and improve, it's vital for businesses to stay up-to-date with the latest advancements and discover new ways to integrate these technologies into their operations. AI holds tremendous potential to revolutionize businesses, and those who can effectively tap into its power are more likely to flourish in an increasingly competitive landscape.

In conclusion, ChatGPT presents an exhilarating opportunity for businesses in the "make money" niche to innovate, automate, and scale their operations. Entrepreneurs and business owners can utilize its capabilities to streamline processes, generate top-notch content, and create winning strategies that catapult their companies to new heights. As technology advances and AI tools like

ChatGPT become even more potent and versatile, the possibilities for growth and success in the "make money" niche are truly boundless.

Manufactured by Amazon.ca
Bolton, ON